PRAISE FOR *FIRST IN, LAST OUT*

"Vivid and outstanding lessons for every leader."

—Warren Bennis, Distinguished Professor of Management,
University of Southern California; coauthor of *Geeks and Geezers*

"*First In, Last Out*'s insightful prescriptions and gripping, firsthand accounts of the FDNY in action make it engaging and instructive, especially for the business manager seeking to develop his or her leadership skills."

—Jason Santamaria and Vincent Marino,
coauthors of *The Marine Corps Way*

"Any organization would love to have the kind of leadership culture exemplified by the FDNY. The wisdom in this book cannot be ignored."

—Patrick Lencioni, best-selling author of
The Five Dysfunctions of a Team and *Death by Meeting*

ABOUT THE AUTHOR

John Salka joined the FDNY in 1979 and rose through the ranks from firefighter to lieutenant, captain, and now battalion chief. He currently leads, manages, and mentors 150 firefighters and 30 officers at his Bronx battalion. He is also the author of many articles on firefighting and leadership techniques. He lives in Orange County, New York, with his wife and five children.

To contact Chief Salka or learn more about his organization, First In Leadership, visit his Web site at www.firstinleadership.com.

Barret Neville is a business editor and writer who lives in New York City.

First In, Last Out

Leadership Lessons from the
New York Fire Department

JOHN SALKA

Batallion Chief, FDNY

WITH BARRET NEVILLE

PORTFOLIO

PORTFOLIO

Published by the Penguin Group

Penguin Group (USA) Inc., 375 Hudson Street, New York, New York 10014, U.S.A.

Penguin Group (Canada), 10 Alcorn Avenue, Toronto, Ontario, Canada M4V 3B2
    (a division of Pearson Penguin Canada Inc.)

Penguin Books Ltd, 80 Strand, London WC2R 0RL, England

Penguin Books Ireland, 25 St Stephen's Green, Dublin 2, Ireland (a division of Penguin Books Ltd)

Penguin Group (Australia), 250 Camberwell Road, Camberwell, Victoria 3124, Australia
    (a division of Pearson Australia Group Pty Ltd)

Penguin Books India Pvt Ltd, 11 Community Centre, Panchsheel Park, New Delhi - 110 017, India

Penguin Group (NZ), cnr Airborne and Rosedale Roads, Albany, Auckland 1310,
    New Zealand (a division of Pearson New Zealand Ltd)

Penguin Books (South Africa) (Pty) Ltd, 24 Sturdee Avenue, Rosebank, Johannesburg 2196, South Africa

Penguin Books Ltd, Registered Offices:
80 Strand, London WC2R 0RL, England

First published in the United States of America by Portfolio, a member of Penguin Group (USA) 2004
This paperback edition published in 2005

10   9   8   7   6   5   4   3   2   1

THE LIBRARY OF CONGRESS HAS CATALOGED THE HARDCOVER EDITION AS FOLLOWS:
Salka, John.
    First in, last out : leadership lessons from the New York Fire Department / John Salka
    and Barret Neville.
        p.   cm.
    Includes bibliographical references and index.
    ISBN 1-59184-025-2 (hc.)
    ISBN 1-59184-068-6 (pbk.)
    1. Leadership.   2. New York (N.Y.). Fire Dept.   I. Neville, Barret.   II. Title.
HM1261.S36   2004
303.3'4—dc22   2003065633

Printed in the United States of America
Set in Spectrum
Designed by Carla Bolte

To my parents, John and Louise Salka, the first real leaders in my life. For their years of guidance, advice, and example that impressed upon me the importance of honesty, integrity, and family.

To my wife, Dawn, and children, John, James, Maureen, Brian, and Colleen, who have endured my hours, days, and weeks of study, travel, and work while I pursued my goals, and who each inspire and motivate me in his or her own special way.

To the members of the FDNY, past, present, and future, who perform the most dangerous and unpredictable job on earth, with pride, enthusiasm, and professionalism. I would like to specifically honor the men of Ladder Company 11, Rescue Company 3, and Squad Company 1, three companies that I was formally assigned to, whose members, as part of the 343 members of the FDNY, were killed in the line of duty, protecting the people of New York and the United States on September 11, 2001.

To Billy, Andy, and Orio, whom I think about every day.

Acknowledgments

We'd both like to thank . . .

The Fire Department of the City of New York, for its cooperation and assistance.

The peerless team at Portfolio, particularly Adrian Zackheim, for his sustaining vision of the book; Will Weisser, for his marketing prowess; and Stephanie Land, for her insightful edits.

A very heartfelt thank-you goes to Bernadette Malone, our editor, whose enthusiasm, graciousness, and sharp talent helped us bring it all together. Joe Perez, for the memorable cover, and Patricia Bozza, for her skillful production editing.

Dennis Smith, for his thoughtful, elegant introduction; and Vincent Dunn, for kicking things off.

And, finally, our agent, Christy Fletcher, who championed the book and whose gentle encouragement made it possible in the first place.

John would like to thank . . .

The people and organizations that have had a positive and lasting effect on my personal and professional development are almost too many to list, but I will try.

I want to thank the officers and members of the Mineola, New York, fire department, where I wore my first helmet and rode my first rig; the Titusville, Florida, fire department, where I collected my first fire service paycheck; and the South Blooming Grove fire department, where I first attained the rank of chief.

My colleagues and friends in the FDNY, especially Mickey Conboy, Fred LaFemina, Mike Dugan, John Keenan, and Jim Murtagh, have been a constant source of inspiration, satisfaction, and admiration during the past twenty-four years and have played a major role in my achievements and contributions to "the job."

Thanks to my friends outside the FDNY who have taught me so much about the things we do, especially Butch Cobb, Mark McLees, and Fred Endrikat.

Many of my most enjoyable and enlightening experiences in the past few years have been while working with the "A" team, my group of friends who are also firefighters, instructors, travel partners, and problem solvers. Thanks to Danny McDonough, Chris Delisio, Miles Gebauer, Rick Tanagretta, and Tom Wutz.

I don't think too many people navigate successfully through life without the assistance and advice of a select group of people, and I am no exception. My inner circle is a small group that has never let me down. Thanks to Jay Jonas, Marty Monaghan, Rich Blatus, and Rick Lasky.

I cannot say thank you without mentioning the officers and members of the companies in the FDNY's 18th Battalion, where I have learned more than I have taught and where I have reaped more than I have sown. Their enthusiasm and professionalism make me prouder than I can express.

Almost every FDNY officer gets promoted through years of studying, and most of them achieve this with a group of other guys that are also studying. My "study group" had a tremendous impact on my career and my rise through the ranks of the FDNY. Thanks, Mike Wilbur, Ralph Fago, Bill Moore, Rich Picciotto, Pete Shovlin, Billy Beyer, Kevin Loughran, and Tony Palazola.

Thanks to Harvey Eisner of *Firehouse* magazine and Bill Manning of

Fire Engineering magazine, who both allow me to occasionally add my two cents to the dialogue of the ever-changing and most noble of professions, firefighting. This book would not be possible without the creative talents of Barry Neville, a fine writer and leader in his own right, whose contributions and concepts are apparent throughout this book and are deeply appreciated.

Barret would like to thank . . .

Laura Tucker, Stefanie Jones, Justin and Sarah D'Ercole, Rich and Kelly Lobel, Mimi O'Connor, Amy and Damian D'Apolito, Patty Leitch, Jennifer Spry, Jeanine Fazio, Marie DiGiorgio, Jeff Rovin, Brian Boucher, Michael Rovin, Shep Boucher, Richard Sillett, and my parents and grandparents (Nevilles, Bautzes, DiSalles, Ruths, and Hoffmans), for their enthusiasm and support.

John Salka, for offering me the chance to work alongside him and witness firsthand the power of a truly generous and inspiring leader.

My wife, Jessica, to whom goes my deepest thanks and love: without you I'd still be staring at a blank page.

Contents

Introduction

"What makes them do it?" is a question I have been asked hundreds of times in the course of my travels through the United States and other parts of the world. It is a natural question. Why do people run into burning buildings that they know just might be the most dangerous locations in the world? It is not by accident that the universally accepted metaphor for hell is an inferno, and no one understands this concept better than our firefighters. Fire is a terrible confrontation, and it is always imminent—it can easily grow to twice its size with every minute an object is aflame. Yet, the firefighters go in. They have a job to do. They are trained and motivated, certainly, but most of all they are led. Who leads them and how do the leaders come to be within the organizational structure of fire departments?

Let me tell you my own story.

There were three goals in my mind that day so many years ago when I first took the oath of office as a New York City fireman (before the term *firefighter* came into common usage). No one had given me that job. I had studied for the intelligence examination, and I had exercised regularly enough to pass the physical test and then some more so I would distinguish myself. But from the moment I was sworn in to the ranks of New York's bravest, I began to feel an indebtedness that

I continue to carry today, for the department placed me among the smartest, most focused, most inspiring leaders that exist in any organization. These men (now men and women) gave me a sense of myself—my capabilities and limitations—that enabled me to succeed at just about anything I have since set my mind to do.

In the beginning of my fire service career I did not think of leadership at all. I did not think about being an officer or a leader. I had no lofty desires. I just took stock in the fact that I was a New York City fireman. I knew that I had the best position in the world, and I was just happy beyond words to be in "the job."

The novice firefighter is called the probie, and when I think back to my days as a probationary fireman, and then through my early years of firefighting, every experience I had and every memory I retain seems to have reinforced the three goals I held as I raised up my hand to be sworn in.

First of all, I wanted to do a good job. I realized I was part of an organization, part of a larger group of firefighters, in which life and death depended on what I did. I knew that mere seconds could often determine if a life was saved or lost—every firefighter internalizes that fact from his first day of training. There is no time to second-guess a decision when fighting a fire. In the emergency services, a course of action has to be right from the moment it is determined, and that takes significant education, training, experience, and a willingness to be certain of and accountable for your decisions. Not many organizations have such an overarching mortal importance in their missions, but that is why the training of leaders in the fire service is so fundamental in its day-to-day operations and so crucial in its consequence. No organization will succeed if it doesn't provide potential leaders with the strong guidelines and mentoring to figure out for him- or herself how to progress positively in a career. In an organization like a fire department, a lack of leadership policy will kill people. I learned all this in the first few days of wearing the uniform, and the structure of the department's management made me feel secure in the nation's most dangerous occupation. I knew my supervisors (the lieutenants, captains, and chief) would do everything possible to keep me focused on my mission and to keep me safe. It was obvious from the beginning that they cared about me, and I wanted to care about them as well. I knew I could do a good job.

My second goal was to be accepted by my peers. It is never easy to be inserted into an established organization, even if you are doing something you have wanted to do for much of your life. You are the new guy on the street, and you want to make friends. But you also want to represent yourself as competent and as an independent thinker. In an organization such as the fire department, though, you have to most of all have a willing mind to be a part of the group. To be of an independent mind while also existing in a group dynamic is a balance that is surprisingly easy to attain in the firehouse, mostly because the organization's shared values—saving lives and property—is so clear. The most fundamental mission for the firefighter is to protect life, a goal that is easily understood when you are taken into a group that has been operating successfully long before you arrived.

True, you do have to prove yourself in the firehouse, and sometimes the firefighters do not make it easy for you. The probationary firefighter is the one who is inevitably asked to go to the store, wash the dishes, sweep the floor, clean the tools, and wash the rig. If he or she dives enthusiastically into the work, the probationary period is painless and relief will come in the support the young firefighter will get from all the senior whips—those who come from "the days of leather hose and wooden fire hydrants." This is the first indication of the leadership mentality that is built into the organization of the fire service. The young, in the firehouse culture, see the value of making themselves willing to learn, as the sage firefighters pass on their secrets in return.

I hated the housecleaning—the ignominy of washing pots and pans when I had trained to save lives. And, I hated being called the probie by everyone. The captain imagined dirt in every corner and on the surface of every tool and ordered me to mop it or polish it. I resented it. Still, I tried to put gusto into every small and insignificant act, and then finally that first fire came. Suddenly, I was on my hands and knees with all the old salts, in the midst of a whirlwind of blinding smoke and searing heat. The captain brought me up to the nozzle, and the senior men backed me up as we went through several rooms of fire in a multiple dwelling. But most important, I felt hands on my back, urging me gently forward, and people all around me finally began calling me Dennis. There is no greater thrill than to be at your first real fire and to be called by your rightful name. The lesson I brought out of the smoking ruin that day is one that I have applied every day since: You can always tell a true leader by the way he treats and teaches the man in the lowest level: the probie.

The third thought in my mind that swearing-in day was simple: I wanted to be the man my mother loved. She spent a lifetime making me ready for school, supporting me during the bad times as well as the good, and advising me with the right information at the right time on countless occasions. Mostly she would say, "You better shape up, kid," which was her way of saying that I was not meeting her expectations—and her expectations were never unreasonable. Trying to be the man my mother loved also means that I wanted to be, then and now, a person who is open and fair to all and who wants to accept every responsibility that comes to the door.

After a lifetime of retrospection, I can now see how vital to my future those early thoughts were. I did not know then, in formulating a list of silent goals, that I was actively involving myself in the leadership program of the New York Fire Department, or that leadership was fundamental to every decision, either in the firehouse or in the middle of a fire. It came with the territory—a territory that had been nurturing courageous men and successful leaders since the fire department was first organized as a paid force in 1865.

Leadership! To want to do a good job was to intuit the life and death nature of firefighting. A fundamental rule in management is that the leader must see clearly the goal of the organization and how to direct people in attaining that goal. The fire department's goal of preserving life and property is constant and shared by everyone from the commissioner to the probie. We don't have to tell people that they can't lead without a shared goal; the instruction is in their very lifestyle.

Leadership! To be accepted by my peers implied that I understood the history and culture of those with whom I rode the back end of a fire pumper. It is difficult to lead people without understanding their past and how they came to be where they are. The fire department has a long list of heroic individuals who have been lost in the line of duty, and with every action in the job, and particularly in the fires, that history is remembered and honored. That historical memory brings with it the motivation to excel, and it supports a rationale that brings men and women to place themselves in mortal danger in the course of their work—and it inspires them to follow their leader.

Leadership! To be the man my mother loved is to apply the integrity I associate with my mother's view of the world to the day-to-day work of the firefighter. Integrity is one of the most important lessons of leadership, and it must be clearly seen in the leader's actions. The actions must be transparent and presented in an environment of intelligence and fairness, and they must be resolute and seen as a commitment. This is a fundamental rule in good leadership, for no one is going to effectively follow a leader he doesn't trust; and in the fire department, all leadership implies trust. This is why the title of this book suggests a leadership style that has worked so effectively in life-and-death situations—the same kind of leadership profile that can be effective in your own organization. To be the first in and last out will earn the trust of all around you and will even inspire some in your organization to greatness. Most important, being first in and last out will define your integrity.

To me there are just two schools of management. There is the knock-'em-over-the-head school, illustrated by the CEO who might say, "All right, this year we are going to send every line manager to Harvard for sensitivity training. . . ." It doesn't take much to see that this "this could work" approach to problem solving is a risky style of management, and one that can be costly. Then there is the more subtle management method, the one in which problem solving is found in the history, culture, values, and experience of the organization, in which the problem-solvers are nurtured in the organization's every-day-and-every-way school of leadership. In this managerial structure, leaders are developed in much the same way we develop our character—it is not something to be learned in a course but developed over a lifetime of doing things in a certain way, the "first in, last out" way.

In the New York Fire Department, a leader is molded by the structure of the job, and John Salka has brought that idea to life within the pages of this important book for all managers. I first met John seven years ago through the pages of *Firehouse* magazine. He was a young captain writing on the subject of management during an emergency scene. I saw him then as an insightful up-and-coming thinker in the fire service. And then, during those tragic and challenging days of Ground Zero, I saw John managing several complicated operations. It was dangerous work. There were many people depending on him. I watched John carefully and worked under his supervision. He was inspiring.

I know that John's influence and reputation at the scene of an emergency will speak to managers in every walk of life who will read this book. You don't have to be operating within a mission where lives are at stake to take value from these pages. You simply have to care about how you manage and want to do better. There are many valuable leadership lessons to be taken away from John Salka's experience and wisdom, but none as great as the one that brings you to be the first one in and the last one out.

Dennis Smith
New York City
September 2003

CHAPTER I

You're the Chief

I've been working on this book for more than twenty years, ever since I stepped down from the cab of 11 Truck's apparatus and came face-to-face with a big fire that was gutting a ConEd plant on Manhattan's Lower East Side. I was a young man then, twenty-two years old, and I was, like all young men, worldly, wise beyond my years, and fearless.

I'd been on the job only a little while, having been appointed back in 1979. After graduating from the academy, I was assigned to 34 Engine, but that was too quiet for me, so I worked the system and got over to 11 Truck, on the Lower East Side. Our firehouse was on East Second Street, between Avenues B and C. Alphabet City. I loved it. I loved everything about being a firefighter. Not only that, but I figured I was getting pretty good at it. I had already made up my mind that there wasn't much a fire could throw at me that I couldn't handle.

The call came in during a day tour. As I said, I was on 11 Truck then, which shared quarters with 28 Engine. Most of the firehouses in New York house two units, both an engine and a truck company. Sometimes you'll hear a truck company referred to as a ladder company. Same thing. In the fire service we refer to the various firehouses by the units they house, so my firehouse at the time was known simply as 28 & 11. Engines carry the hose and pump the water, and the firefighters who man the engine rig are the ones who'll stretch the hose to the location of the fire and literally crawl right into the room that's burning and smother the flames beneath water that exits the nozzle like a pile driver, at three hundred gallons per minute. The ladder company firefighters, or truckies, force open doors, vent windows, cut the roof, and perform search-and-rescue. These two units complement each other perfectly; together, they manage all the key jobs that must be accomplished to fight a fire successfully.

On the day the call came in, I was the junior man on 11 Truck. Most of the other men in the company had worked there for years, and being the new guy, I was usually assigned one of the positions, like the can or irons, that for safety and training reasons would keep me close to the officer. Wherever that officer went, I went. In addition, all around me were some of the best firefighters in the city. I could learn more from them in a day than in an entire week at the Fire Academy.

I had grown up in the quiet suburbs of Long Island, so the neighborhood around 11 Truck seemed almost exotic to me, and as we'd go to and from calls, I was mesmerized by the endless rows of bodegas that flew past as we raced down Avenue B, or the blocks of vacant tenement buildings that stood quietly by as we shot along the streets of the Lower East Side. But it wasn't even the buildings I was interested in, so much as the people. This was 1981, a time when this neighborhood was sort of a freaky place, known mainly for its drug addicts and bohemian types, a combination that provided plenty to look at.

Lately, however, I'd decided to start acting like the hardened fireman I was sure I was becoming, and now, riding to the call, I didn't even bother to look up from my gear. I imagined myself a seasoned smoke eater, just taking care of business. But then we pulled up at the fire, and suddenly I felt like it was my first day on the job again.

The fire was at the ConEdison building on Fourteenth Street, near the East River. We were the second-due truck there, after 3 Ladder (second-due means we arrived after 3 Ladder; our job was to back them up), so several other units were already there when we pulled up. As I hopped down from the apparatus, the first thing I noticed about this building was its size. It was gigantic. It sprawled across an entire block, and its thick walls stretched high above the sidewalk. There were hardly any windows. Looking up from the foot of the building, I saw nothing but the sheer concrete wall, and then the sky; but from across the street I could see the smokestacks rising above the power plant like watchtowers. Here was a fortress at the edge of the East River, and somewhere inside it was a fire. Smoke was in the air.

Although there was obviously a serious problem inside the plant, things were not moving that quickly. Usually, in ordinary fires (if there is such a thing), companies arrive and instantly go to work in their assigned areas. These assignments are predetermined and well known to every firefighter on every rig. The first engine and truck to arrive go to the fire floor. The second truck company reports to the floor above, to search for people trapped by the flames. The second engine assists the first engine, and so forth. These jobs apply to a fire in a multiple-residence dwelling (MD). There are other configurations for different types of MDs, as well as for private homes and commercial buildings, but there was no specific protocol for the ConEd plant.

Since we were second-due, we "stood fast," or waited with our apparatus as our officers got a handle on the incident and worked out a strategy. The chief was talking to the ConEd people, trying to gather as much information as possible before putting companies into the building. At the same time, engines were connecting to hydrants, truck chauffeurs were positioning their apparatus for access to the building, and both officers and firefighters were assembling with tools, Scott Air Packs, radios, and other equipment, ready to go to work.

Now, this particular fire turned out to be a hydrogen fire, an oddball kind of fire, and there's nothing that puts a guy on edge like a fire he's never seen before. We really couldn't see the beast yet, and the ConEd people had been a little sketchy about what exactly was wrong, but we could clearly identify the sharp cracks and deep roaring sound so common to large conflagrations. Everyone was a little nervous; you could see it in the looks we exchanged with one another, the way some of us fumbled around with our equipment, the sudden silence that fell over us.

Approaching the fire, its heat lunging at us, we could dimly see a huge cylindrical tank at the inferno's core. Superheated by the frenzy all around it, its contents were making a tremendous noise—a shrill, piercing whistle that made you, the instant you heard it, just want to get the hell out of there.

While I can't say exactly what the other guys were thinking or feeling, I know what hit me as I stared at that snarling orange whirlwind. It was fear, but not like any I'd experienced before. It was a cold, coiling fear that took my breath away. By some unspoken consensus, we had slowed almost to a halt when our lieutenant turned around, looked each of us in the eye, and said, "Follow me." Turning around, without looking to see if we were behind him, he plunged toward the flames. And we followed.

"First in, last out." That sums up the leadership code of the FDNY. Like most other leadership principles, it's a simple concept, but one that's difficult to live up to. Company officers are expected to be the first into every fire and the last to leave. It's our duty to expose ourselves to the same risks we ask our guys to take. It's part of the sacred trust that exists between officers and firefighters. "First in, last out" encompasses key leadership qualities like integrity, commitment, focus, and intensity. Even Mayor Fiorello La Guardia, one of New York City's greatest mayors (and greatest fire buffs), knew that this was the key to leadership. In response to critics who complained that he spent more time at fires than at City Hall, La Guardia asked, "[What] would the men think if I didn't have the guts to go where they went, especially if there was danger?"

Since that day as the junior man on 11 Truck, I've observed many different styles of leadership. I've also had many chances to develop my own, first as a lieutenant, then as a captain, and finally as the chief of Battalion 18, in the Bronx. At the moment, I'm responsible for the lives of 150 firefighters and countless more citizens. On the apparatus floor of my Bronx firehouse is 58 Truck, a brand-new Seagrave tower ladder apparatus. Weighing several tons, it's a squat, pug-nosed beast wrapped in the gleaming red-and-white colors of the FDNY. Even when fully extended, its ninety-five-foot boom (or ladder) can withstand the strain of the thousand gallons per minute being directed by the firefighter perched in its bucket—a tremendous force that can actually overturn a truck that's not properly stabilized. In the bay next door is 45 Engine. Like its neighbor, this Seagrave pumper is low, heavy, and specially modified for the FDNY's unique needs. It can deliver a thousand gallons of water per minute from its pumps, while the rear hose bed offers room for nearly a half ton of hose. Together, the apparatuses represent a $1 million investment by New York City. And there are two more firehouses within my battalion, each housing a similar engine-and-truck one-two punch.

In addition to serving in traditional, hierarchical leadership roles (such as lieutenant and captain), it's my privilege to have had many different leadership opportunities. I've taught probies at the academy. I've created special training programs that help firefighters adapt to the changing realities of our work. I was one of original covering officers selected to work in the newly created Special Operations Command. I helped manage the recovery effort at Ground Zero. But mainly what I've done is watch how officers in the FDNY—the Fire Department of the City of New York—lead their people. Over the past twenty years I've learned about leadership from people whose bravery, honor, and dedication are a constant inspiration to me.

Not all my leadership role models have come from within the department, however. It's not like we hold the secret formula or something. But that's the great thing about leadership: you find worthwhile examples of it in all industries and organizations. Great leaders everywhere draw on the same principles and strategies to accomplish their goals. There are things I can learn from a business leader about motivation, just as there are things I can teach that leader about execution.

But I can't tell you my leadership story, or even the story of leadership in the FDNY, without talking for a second about organizations themselves—those environments within which leadership is exercised. Organizations have always been society's best way of achieving its various goals. If you don't believe me, just stop and take a closer look at the world around you: organizations define, measure, and direct the flow of our everyday lives. Profit, nonprofit, or government agency, every organization exists in order to accomplish some objective that can't be achieved through individual effort. The father of modern management, Peter Drucker, called organizations "the organs of society." Which, of course, is very true. Organizations are not created to serve themselves but to serve the communities within which they exist.

The FDNY is no different. All told, it's an organization comprising 8,599 firefighters, 2,629 officers, 203 engine companies, 143 truck companies, 7 squads, 5 rescue companies, 3 marine companies, and a hazmat company. I think those are pretty impressive statistics, and I know the department loves them dearly. And why not? They describe a strong organization, staffed by able, intelligent, and resourceful men and women with vast material resources at their disposal.

But I always find myself more interested in another set of numbers. The "New York" part of FDNY is a constant reminder of our responsibility to the people of this great city. And New York doesn't mean just that stuff in the "I Love NY" commercials, but all of New York City, every square mile of that great, teeming metropolis composed of Manhattan, Brooklyn, Queens, the Bronx, and Staten Island, with its 8 million people and three hundred square miles of skyscrapers, apartment buildings, waterfront, warehouses, industrial complexes, and homes.

Whenever I contemplate that other set of numbers—the New York City set—I feel great pride in the FDNY's accomplishments. But the inequality of the two sets of statistics—I mean, you've got this one relatively miniscule organization responsible for the safety of one of the world's biggest cities—points to the importance of the one thing that makes organizations work: leadership.

Leadership is what makes organizations effective. It's the essential spark that makes things happen. The same kind of leadership that creates successful corporations also makes nonprofits more productive, nations more vigorous, and armies more powerful. It also makes hospitals more effective and teachers more inspiring. Without leadership, an organization is just a loosely connected group of people operating without a unifying focus or coordinating mission, pursuing different goals, flailing in a hundred sometimes contradictory directions. In fact, one of the most useful things that came out of the so-called New Economy was proof of the necessity of leadership. The notions that new technologies had made leadership and management obsolete, that self-directed work teams would replace the traditional organizational structures, and that everyone could be "self-managing" were exposed as a load of bull.

In short, organizations need leaders because leaders unify groups of people through mutually held values and goals and help them to achieve common objectives. That's my personal definition—there are others out there, but they all boil down to the same thing: leadership makes organizations work. Leadership guides and directs, it prioritizes and orients, it teaches and develops. It processes information and makes it useful. It strategizes and plans, envisions and dreams. Let me break it down even more: since organizations need leaders in order to function, and since we've already discussed how organizations make our society work, you don't have to go very far to see that leadership itself is an important force in our world.

I think it's this idea of leadership as a creative force that makes what passes for leadership today even more depressing. I'm thinking, of course, of the leaders of Enron, Tyco, Arthur Anderson, and Health-South, and the scores of others who have embroiled their companies in scandal or fraud.

But how well does my definition of leadership hold up in the real world? Let's take another look at it: *Leaders unify groups of people through mutually held values and goals and help them to achieve common objectives.* Hmm. According to my definition, even someone like Ken Lay is a leader. Didn't he rally his Enronites around the goal of making lots of money any way they could? And didn't he establish a value system (that is, "Anything goes") that permitted them to do whatever it took to achieve that goal? If someone succeeds in working through his people to achieve commonly held objectives (no matter what they are), then he's a leader, right? But something in your gut disagrees with this. I know something in mine does. It just seems wrong.

So if my gut's at all accurate, leadership means something more than just achieving goals through others. To really talk about leadership in a meaningful way, we need to come up with a way to talk about it that passes our gut test. For instance, I like Drucker's idea that all organizations exist to serve society, and therefore leaders have to concern themselves with the social impacts and social responsibilities of their organizations.

Using that idea as a jumping-off point, here's what I think makes a great leader: not only do you have to work with your people to enable them to make good things happen for your organization, but you've got to take into account the goals and values of all the people your organization touches, from your shareholders to your employees to your customers to the larger community that may be affected by your actions. I don't put this out there lightly; it's a big responsibility. But the important thing is that, as a leader, you recognize this responsibility and strive to meet it.

At the moment, our country faces enormous crises, and I don't think it's an overstatement to say that the character of our response will shape the world for generations to come. And as if the shocks of the new century weren't enough—the threat of terrorists and rogue nations, of companies that have misled the very society they were meant to serve, of an uncertain global environment—we're still struggling with those old standbys of racism, poverty, disease, and war. We hear about solutions to these conundrums (usually around election time), solutions that are always touted as the "answer." Sometimes these answers appear as a new patent, or a new piece of legislation, or a new treaty, or a military victory. But in reality, there is only one answer to these problems, and that's leadership.

I've been pondering and studying leadership—both firsthand and on the printed page—ever since that day as the junior man on 11 Truck. Subsequent promotions only sharpened my desire (and quite frankly, my need) to know everything there was to know about leading people effectively. Of course, I don't have all the answers, but my experiences as a leader in this very successful, world-famous organization have certainly given me access to insights, wisdom, and practical strategies that I hope will prove valuable to other leaders, across all organizations and at all levels of development.

Because I feel that as a leader, you're never *done*, I've always tried to read as many leadership books as I can. I prowl the business section of the bookstores, and when a new one comes out, I snatch it up. And I'm rarely disappointed. I almost always learn something new, or rediscover something I'd forgotten, or gain a new perspective on an old challenge.

But here's the thing that bugs me. A lot of these books seem to assume that you're either a CEO or on the verge of becoming one, and that there are only a handful of leaders in the world—a small group (all men, by the way) who answer to the names Jack Welch, Michael Dell, Bill Gates, or if you're into history, maybe Gandhi, George Patton, and Abraham Lincoln. Now, I truly believe that each of these men is or was a great leader, and that there is a tremendous amount to be learned from examining how they led their people through some extremely challenging situations. That said, I've always felt that it's a shame we never get to hear from the department supervisor in Houston who's discovered ways to double the productivity of her people, or the manager in Sacramento whose team leads the company in money-saving innovations, or even, yes, the FDNY captain who knows how to get the job done no matter how big and ugly it is. Even if I don't know all of these people's names, I can guarantee that they do exist, and that there are many more like them.

Unlike CEOs or other top executives, these leaders don't have the power to set strategy, reorganize the corporation, or implement a brand-new vision that will lead the company into the next century. But just like CEOs, they perform all the basic functions of a leader:

- They guide people's efforts toward a common goal.
- They leverage their organization's traditions, culture, and values to unify people in a common cause.
- They help people grow and develop through teaching and mentoring.
- They forge effective relationships with people that allow for clear communication of goals, priorities, and expectations.

So I set out to write the kind of straight-talking book I've always wanted to read, one that offered practical leadership insights to leaders at all levels, from the frontline supervisor to the CEO.

The most essential of these insights, "first in, last out," is the foundation of FDNY leadership and encompasses such vital areas as building trust, opening communications, emphasizing transparency, and working alongside your people. But before we begin to explore how you can put "first in, last out" leadership to work for you, the first few chapters will focus on some issues that might seem somewhat theoretical at first. They stress the need to take a look at yourself and your organization before jumping in and trying to lead from the front—after all, you have to know where *you're* headed before you try to lead others.

In the next couple of hundred pages you'll discover some new insights into leadership and also gain a fresh perspective on some established principles. In addition, you'll find straightforward strategies and techniques that you can apply to the big leadership questions: How can I get my people to do what I want them to? How can I make sure the right thing gets done? How can I make sure we're doing the right things in the first place? And finally, how can I get the most out of my people?

The story of the FDNY is, at heart, the story of an organization whose tradition of phenomenal leadership has always enabled it to meet and overcome any challenge, no matter how daunting. Whether you're a small business owner or a CEO, a frontline supervisor or a top executive, I hope that the example of the FDNY and its corps of leaders will inspire and guide you as you continue on your leadership journey. You may not know it, or perhaps you may not want to admit it to yourself, but you have the power to create a positive change, even if it's just in your particular "firehouse."

Remember, you're the chief.

CHAPTER 2

The Leadership Triangle

What is the foundation of great leadership?

Though we tend to blame fires on a single thing, like a naked wire, a stray spark, or a lit match, in actuality fire has three essential elements: heat, oxygen, and fuel. The three points of this triangle interact to form the chain reaction that leads to combustion. In the same way, leadership is not sparked by any one thing, such as charisma or presence or rank, but is built on a foundation created by three *leadership commitments*.

These commitments are not inborn virtues, techniques, or skills. They're disciplines that you've got to learn. And that's good news, because it means any of us can master them. All it takes is constant attention and effort. "First in, last out" leadership is hard work, but I can guarantee that if you truly apply yourself, and do your best to honor this leadership triangle, you'll be able to reach your full potential.

Many leadership failures actually result from an unwillingness to face the true nature of a situation. Think, for example, of how the American auto industry almost went out of business in the 1970s after ignoring consumers' demands for smaller, more fuel-efficient cars. The auto manufacturers' refusal to acknowledge the reality of their business environment (higher gas prices, environmental concerns) and the demands of the customers led them to the brink of disaster.

That's why the first commitment has to be to *reality*. You've got to be relentless in going after the truth, no matter what.

The second commitment is to *treating your people as assets*. Or to put it another way, it's a commitment to stop looking at your people as just plain, old, ordinary people and instead to start seeing them in a new light: as the engines that drive your organization.

The third and final commitment is to *developing leaders at all levels of your organization*. This is probably the most challenging of the three, and to make it happen you'll need to draw on a number of different leadership competencies. However, it's also the most powerful: with it, you'll be able to expand your influence throughout your organization and help move it in the right direction.

FOLLOW THE SMOKE

Sometimes we refer to fire as the Beast or the Demon—not out of some misplaced sense of the melodramatic, but because sometimes it behaves like something that's trying really hard to kill us. It can lurk undiscovered in the basement, chewing away at the floor beneath us. It can travel unseen inside the walls. It can leap across fifty-foot gaps between buildings or across a four-lane thoroughfare. It can fester inside a closed room, ready to explode in the face of the first firefighter to step through the door.

While we firefighters may not always be able to see the fire right away, we know, like any good hunter, how to track it. Smoke is the key. From its color and smell, an experienced firefighter can tell you what kind of substance is fueling a fire and how long it's been burning. From the volume of smoke, we can sometimes tell how advanced the burn is. But most important, by following the smoke we can find and fight the fire itself.

I just want to make one thing clear: the smoke itself is not what we're after. We want the fire. Smoke is simply a symptom of that fire, a kind of information or a clue that reveals what we need to know about our target. We never mistake smoke for fire.

So what do I mean when I tell you, "Follow the smoke"? Simply that as a leader, you not only need to remain alert to the unique kinds of smoke you'll encounter in your business or organization, but you need to remember not to mistake that smoke for the fire. The smoke is only a clue. Remember that and let it lead you to the underlying issues.

For example, say that you discover that your people are hiding information from you. Now, by itself this may seem like a problem. But it's really just a symptom of a more fundamental issue. In other words, it's smoke.

Some managers might settle for fighting the smoke, either by ordering their people to keep them in the loop or by trying to impose some new process designed to free up information. But great leaders know better than to fight the smoke. They follow it, trying to find the fire—the underlying problem. They probe, investigate, and question. They try to figure out if people are hiding information because (a) they're afraid they'll be punished for their candor (the "killing the messenger" effect) or (b) they don't understand the importance of sharing information or (c) they're trying to cover up their own errors. Once these leaders discover the true issue, they can nip the whole thing in the bud. They know that had they settled for fighting the smoke, it would be only a matter of time before another problem, caused by the same unaddressed, underlying issues, took its place.

Following the smoke means not settling for what's right in front of you. It means uncovering and embracing what's *really* going on, no matter how painful that may be. It means not allowing fear, bias, or ambition to blind you to the real issues in your organization or industry.

Failing to follow the smoke can have disastrous consequences. In my line of work it can mean that people will die. The stakes are probably not quite that high for you, but they're still important. For example, if you fail to probe for and uncover what's really going on in your industry, you'll miss the new trends and innovations that are changing your business's landscape. Your organization will never have a chance to account for those changes, and eventually they'll overwhelm you. In fact, Ram Charan and Larry Bossidy, in their book *Execution*, make a point of urging leaders to be realistic about their business assumptions and to always monitor their environment for changes that might affect them.

Refusing to commit to reality is just as hazardous on an interpersonal level. When a leader is blind to how *his own* nature impacts his people, he makes his team or even the entire organization a hostage to his irrational impulses and destructive behavior. We've all worked with bullies, micromanagers, and others whose behavior suppresses cooperation, enthusiasm, and the free flow of ideas and information. The decreased engagement of employees and the lower rates of productivity and effectiveness that result from these behaviors are every bit as deadly to your organization as an out-of-control blaze is to mine.

"Follow the smoke" is just another way of saying, "Look for the right information." As I constantly tell the officers I mentor, information is essential to leadership. There are two different kinds of information: *quantitative*, that is, numbers, raw data, things that can be measured and standardized; and *qualitative*, that is, more subjective kinds of information, like observation and opinion. Just as you need both the creative and the analytical halves of your brain to function as a complete person, you need both kinds of information to understand reality.

For example, up until mid-2001, the FDNY had been working on implementing a ComStat program modeled after the NYPD's system. ComStat involved collecting mountains of data, analyzing it, and then packaging it to be used during meetings between the upper-echelon department officers (basically, the FDNY's corporate office) and the field commanders (the department heads and frontline managers). The goal of the program was to uncover trends and problems that could be addressed early on, thereby improving the service we provide to the community, our customers. In reality, however, the program's meetings came to be perceived by the field commanders as a more or less scripted events; the ComStat data was king, and the commanders' qualitative observations and personal insights were marginalized. This overemphasis on quantitative data meant that the higher-ups in the department weren't getting the whole story. In other words, they didn't have all the information they needed to lead effectively. We've since shelved the ComStat experiment, though it may return in some modified form in the future.

The moral of this story is worth emphasizing now more than ever. Computers have become essential to fire operations, just as they have in almost every other organization. However, this means there are lots of leaders out there who have access to an abundance of quantitative data, but who perhaps don't spend much time talking to their people, gathering opinions and observations, or simply getting out from behind their desks and walking around. Relying too much on one kind of information over the other will deprive you of the big picture and limit your effectiveness as a leader.

Finding the Smoke

Before you can follow the smoke, you need to find it. But how exactly do you do that? And once you do find it, what strategies can you use to find the underlying issues, the reality, that the smoke points to? While there are no easy answers to these questions, there are a few guidelines that will help you stay on track. After being mentored by great officers and leading some of the best firefighters in the world, I've been able to identify the following five principles to help you find out what's really going on within yourself, your organization, and your industry.

Identify Your Emotional Triggers

Leaders need to stay in control, not just of their organizations but of themselves and their emotions. Sometimes you yourself are the reason why things aren't working. In this case, your emotions are the smoke, so start by monitoring them. Why your emotions? Because by riding herd on your emotions you can find the triggers that cause you to overreact or behave in ways that undermine your own leadership. Triggers are those parts of our nature that are so sensitive to certain kinds of input that they override our more or less rational selves. For example, for me sarcasm is a trigger; a sarcastic response from one of my firefighters is liable to make me turn red in the face and perhaps fly off the handle.

Understanding your triggers is key, because once you recognize them you can begin to manage them. We all know what it's like to overreact. We've all been in situations where we've responded irrationally, becoming furious, fearful, indignant, or even panicky, without good reason. Learn to treat these unreasonable reactions as the smoke; any kind of unreasonable emotional flare-up should be a clue that the current situation has somehow aggravated one of your triggers. Armed with this knowledge, you can start working to uncover the deeper issues within yourself that are provoking this self-sabotaging response and begin to manage them.

Information Is Like Water at a Fire: More Is Better

In addition to facing the truth about themselves, leaders need to uncover the truth about their organizations or industries. Like that wisp of smoke that ultimately leads us to the fire, the right piece of information can help you find the weaknesses in your organization that keep it from reaching its full potential, or the new trends in the marketplace that could give you a first-mover advantage.

My job, the second I hit the fire ground, is to get a handle on the big picture, what's really going on. We usually tear out of the firehouse, sirens blasting, knowing nothing more about what awaits us than an address or an alarm-box number. We don't know the type of structure, the location of the fire, or what has started the blaze. So as soon as my boots hit the pavement and the smoke hits my nostrils, I start gathering information. Some of it is quantitative data, such as the type of building involved (is it a tenement, a warehouse, a high-rise?), the kinds of materials that were used in the construction, the temperature at which they combust, and their characteristic burn pattern. And some of it's observational. For example, I'll examine the fire in order to gauge its progress: How is the fire moving? Is it extending to the exposures? Have the windows shattered from the heat? What color is the smoke? What can I learn from its odor? I'll send firefighters to check out all four exposures of a building, as well as any adjoining structures, in order to map the progression of a fire. Only after I have all this info can I begin formulating a strategy for attacking and subduing the fire.

The key to being a successful leader is making sure you get acquainted with as many different types of smoke (that is, information) as possible. The more varied your info, in terms of sources and types of data, the greater your chances of arriving at the optimal outcome. So what can you do to make sure you're getting the right mix of information?

Start by analyzing your sources, particularly those on which you base key assumptions that affect your organization. Ask yourself questions. Are you getting your news live from the front lines, or is it twisting its way through the organization, reaching you so massaged and sanitized that it's practically useless? Do you get updates from a number of different subordinates, or do you rely on only a chosen few for your daily productivity report?

Ask Your People, Because They Know the Answer

FDNY officers are noted for carefully observing and assessing a situation before making any decisions. Obviously, we can't be everywhere at once, or personally investigate every aspect of what's going on. So how do we collect enough information to put together a coherent picture of the situation? By getting out and talking to our people, the men and women who are personally involved with all the various aspects of the operation. We borrow their knowledge and insights to help us put together a more complete and useful version of reality. Before making key decisions, we talk to our subordinate officers, our experts, and our frontline people. We know that our people have all the answers, even if they don't know they do. Or to put it another way, they have the raw materials (the information) but need a leader to put it all together and make something useful out of it. We know that the guys in the thick of the blaze are the best source of information to tap when we're trying to see a situation for what it really is.

Have the Courage to Face the Smoke

So by now you know that the first commitment involves some hard work, but did you know it's also one of the most courageous things a leader can do? I mean, I've got a ton of great stories about guys who have put themselves in mortal danger to get the job done, but it takes a special kind of fortitude to dare to uncover information that might upset the status quo or challenge the majority.

A few years ago, Vincent Dunn, a deputy chief with the FDNY, responded to a two-alarm fire up in Harlem, at 125th Street and Eighth Avenue. As a deputy chief, which is the next rank above mine (battalion chief), Dunn was responsible for an entire division—that is, a sector of the city comprising a handful of battalions. Because deputy chiefs respond to all serious fires in their divisions, which can be quite a large area, they tend to arrive a little after the excitement has started and the engine and truck companies have already deployed under the direction of the battalion chief.

However, when Dunn arrived on the scene he found that not only had the FDNY companies already engaged the fire, but the building—a two-story commercial structure that was pretty heavily involved with flames—was surrounded by cops wearing body armor and carrying shotguns and bulletproof shields. This was not only a fire, it was a hostage situation. The building within which the gunman was holding his hostages was showing flame out of the upstairs windows—usually a sign of an advanced fire—and firefighters had begun attacking the blaze even as police officers maneuvered to capture the gunman.

Dunn quickly found the battalion chief. As their men continued to push the two-and-a-half-inch attack lines into the building, and the water from each nozzle bored into the inferno at the rate of 250 gallons per minute, and aerial ladders were thrust toward the roof, Dunn got to work learning all he could about the situation. After listening carefully to everything the battalion chief and the other officers could tell him about the fire, Dunn pondered what to do. As he thought through his various possible strategies, EMS teams hustled past him carrying gunshot victims covered in blood.

Dunn knew that there was no SOP (standard operating procedure) for a situation like this. While you might think it's crazy that he would decide to hang around while the cops and the gunman played gunfight at the OK Corral, the FDNY's mission—to save lives—was foremost in Dunn's mind. Clearly, that mission was applicable here. There were a number of people being held in that building, and even if they survived the gunman, the flames and choking smoke would certainly kill them. What's more, the firefighters were already committed to the attack. Another officer had just radioed Dunn from the rear of the building, requesting permission to do a search of the basement.

The easy thing to do would be to press the attack against the flames. All of Dunn's training, his sense of duty and mission, and even his men urged him to maintain the pressure on the fire. But to his great credit he had already grasped the reality of the situation. He recalled thinking: The gunman could be forced out of the building, shooting wildly; then the police would shoot back, and the bodies of firefighters could be lying all over the sidewalk. Dunn made his decision. He ordered his firefighters to fall back, and requested two more tower ladders to lay down a curtain of water and make sure the fire didn't spread to adjacent buildings.

Later it was discovered that seven of the hostages had died from smoke inhalation. Dunn had some rough nights after that, but ultimately he decided that he'd made the only possible choice, given the situation.

This is exactly what I mean when I say that leadership becomes most valuable in extreme situations. Without the courage to face the reality of the scene, Dunn might have just given in to the momentum of events and allowed the firefighters to continue battling the fire. It would have been the easy thing to do. But instead he had the courage to see the situation for what it was and make the hard choice. It wasn't easy but it was right.

I can't tell you how to be courageous. But I can tell you what it looks like—courage is being the first one through that smoke-filled hallway or a fiery entryway, and the last one to come back out again.

Never Be Too Busy Leading to Teach

How can serving as a teacher to your people help you follow the smoke and uncover reality? First of all, the very nature of teaching requires you to be in close contact with employees. While you can manage people from a distance through e-mail and memos—sort of—those methods won't work when it comes to teaching. Teaching forces you to get out among your people and talk to them. Teaching creates a kind of give-and-take between teacher and student that encourages the free exchange of ideas and information, which means that through teaching you can access your people's expertise, observations, and insights. In other words, through teaching you'll end up with a lot more information to work with when you're trying to get a handle on what's really happening in your organization or industry.

Another way to describe the give-and-take of the teaching relationship is as a teaching-and-learning dynamic. In other words, to be open to teaching one must also be open to learning. This is an important point because, as a leader, you're never finished growing and developing. I hate to say it, but as long as you continue to occupy a leadership role, you'll never be able to kick back, click on the TV, and think to yourself, Well, that's it; I'm done. This is particularly true whenever the first commitment comes into play. Only by continuing to learn and develop will you be sure to have the tools and perspective you need to ask the right questions, to recognize reality when you finally uncover it, and finally, to know how best to use the knowledge or insights you've gained to lead your people in achieving your organization's goals.

This is just a brief overview of how the first commitment can support your leadership mission in a number of key areas, from long-term planning to day-to-day interactions. I really can't overstate its importance. You can be a great leader in every other way; you can have unsurpassed communications skills and a superhuman ability to inspire and motivate; you can be master of the execution-oriented decision and exhibit a knowledge of high strategy that would shame Sun-tzu, but if you don't have a commitment to reality, then all your stupendous talents will be applied in the wrong places, and the ultimate result will unfortunately be characterized as a failure of leadership.

DON'T TREAT YOUR PEOPLE LIKE PEOPLE, TREAT THEM LIKE ASSETS

"In today's world, a company's people are its most important value-producing assets." This quote, from Noel Tichy, breaks my heart. It really does. Not because I think Professor Tichy is wrong, but because I know he's right. He's right, and yet it seems that the majority of organizations out there are just paying lip service to the idea he's enunciating. The worst offenders are those organizations—and their leaders—that insist on calling their people "strategic assets" or "competitive advantages," while at the same time stifling them with rules, regulations, and mind-numbing bureaucracies.

Personally, I think organizations and leaders stumble when it comes to their people because they get hung up on the idea that valuing their people means making them *feel* valued, as opposed to treating them as assets that *create* value. Most organizations have responded to the urgings of Tichy, Peter Drucker, and others by enshrining the "People are assets" concept in their mission statements, and therein lies the problem. Statements like "Our people are our most important asset" don't require you to do anything. It's an empty platitude, not a call to action.

And when leaders do try to practice the idea that "people are the most important part of an organization," they take it to mean that they should work on making their people happier or more fulfilled. This also misses the point. Companies end up trying to show their people how much they appreciate them with things like pizza Fridays or summer outings, instead of figuring out how they can get the most out of these underutilized assets. I could treat everyone in the firehouse to steak dinners, except that free steaks are not going to make them better or happier firefighters. But when I give them the freedom to do their jobs and apply their considerable talents in the way they see fit, they're the most effective, most motivated bunch you've ever seen.

The truth is, your people don't want you to treat them like people, or employees for that matter. Because hey, you may treat employees badly, but you'll never mistreat assets that make it possible for you to do your job. Even a lousy manager will ensure that the assets that make the organization successful—from factories to patents—are well cared for. Whether it's making sure that these assets have the resources they need to be effective, or that their environments allow them to run at peak efficiency, he'll do everything he can to create a situation where they can perform at optimal levels. His organization's success depends on them.

The Power Is in Your People

Because we fire officers spend most of our careers out on the front line with the men and women of our companies, battalions, and divisions, we know that it's our people who get the work done. And as much as we may like our expensive equipment—our thermal imagers and high-altitude gear and rescue rigs—we know that unless there's a firefighter at the nozzle end of that hose, crouched beneath the scorching, one-thousand-degree smoke rolling out of that doorway, there's no way that fire gets knocked down. That firefighter is our primary asset. All the other stuff is just to help him be even more effective.

Our people have always been our primary means of success. The forebears of the FDNY were the citizens of New Amsterdam, as New York was then called. Back in the late 1600s, firefighting was everyone's responsibility. When the night watch sounded the alarm, people were expected to throw leather buckets out into the street, where the citizen firefighters would gather them up and stretch a bucket brigade down to the Fresh Pond (now vanished beneath the bricks and stone of Lower Manhattan). Others would take up long hooks and begin pulling down fiery walls to keep the blaze from spreading.

In those days, people were the *only* assets. They were willing to sacrifice their lives, not just for others but—and this was particularly true in 1600s New Amsterdam, where one good fire could wipe out an entire community—to preserve civilization itself. Even as the equipment grew more sophisticated and the emergencies more dangerous, only that most important asset, people, could make the equipment useful and could respond creatively to unforeseen perils.

In the FDNY, we've never forgotten those early days. We treat our people as assets, first, by recognizing how important they are to the success of the mission. We do this by training with them daily and teaching them the new skills necessary to respond to emergencies in a changing world. We mentor them and help them develop. Second, we make sure their work atmosphere is conducive to doing effective work. New York City firehouses are somewhat famous for their collegial, upbeat atmosphere, and we encourage that. Third, we make sure our people stay healthy and fit; we always want to make sure our assets are in optimal condition. Finally, we offer them strong, capable leadership, which is no less than our assets deserve.

Keep Your Assets in Working Condition

As with the commitment to reality, much of what makes a leader successful in making the transition from regarding his people as people—idiosyncratic, unpredictable, often frustrating—to regarding them as assets that he relies on to get where he's going is the will to do so.

There's certainly no secret to it. In addition to being aware of how you interact with your employees, you can help them by doing the same things you'd do for any other asset on which your success depends. For example, put people in positions where they can do the things they're best at, and don't ask them to do work that they're not suited for. Cultivate an environment where they're comfortable, and one that helps them be effective. Don't set them up for failure. Make sure they have the tools and resources they need to accomplish the organization's goals. And always provide strong direction.

DEVELOP LEADERS AT ALL LEVELS

In his Pulitzer Prize–winning book, *Leadership,* James MacGregor Burns wrote that leaders need to help their followers become leaders as well, since "only by standing on *their* shoulders can true greatness in leadership be achieved." Even before Burns put it in writing, however, successful organizations such as General Electric, IBM, and the FDNY had made a rule of encouraging people throughout their organizations to adopt leadership roles. By developing leaders at all levels, you amplify the effectiveness of your leadership actions and enable your messages and initiatives to reach into every corner of the organization.

But what does this commitment really mean? Let's think about it for a second or two. *Leaders at all levels*—not only does it sound like some kind of nutty management fantasy, but isn't there a saying, "Too many cooks spoil the soup"? You're the leader, after all. Do you really want people questioning your decisions, substituting their own way for your way, going off in new directions based solely on their own interpretation of organizational objective?

The answer is yes, that's exactly what you want. But developing leaders at all levels doesn't mean inaugurating a mad power grab in the hallways and cubicles of your company. So what exactly does the third commitment look like in action?

If there's one image that exemplifies this concept, it's that of an organization where everyone models the three leadership commitments and where each person defines his or her role in terms of our leadership definition. By encouraging your people to think of themselves as leaders, you'll find that they become more deeply engaged in the work, take accountability for their performance, and stay focused on the organization's goals. People will orient their activities around outcomes rather than processes or arbitrary measurements, and this new perspective will stimulate their creativity and generate a flood of valuable innovations that will make your organization more competitive, effective, and successful.

Despite my enthusiasm for cultivating leaders at all levels—and the fact that I can personally attest to its power after having seen it work throughout the FDNY—I still find it hard sometimes to sell people on the concept. I think part of the problem lies with our popular notions of leadership. As I've said before, being a leader is not about occupying an office or holding a title. It's not a specific occupation, rank, or job description. Leadership is just a name for what happens when someone uses certain actions and attitudes to work through people to achieve common goals. Anyone can practice leadership, from CEOs down to entry-level employees.

General Electric is an excellent example of a company that thrives on homegrown leadership. After Jack Welch took over at GE, he made leadership development a priority. He believed his job was to know and develop people, as opposed to immersing himself in the details of GE's many businesses. "Every day," he explained, "we are developing and assessing people, in the hallway, in meetings, at Crotonville [GE's leadership development center], on the job, trying them in new jobs." The success of his approach is evident in the value other organizations have placed on the results of his leadership philosophy: in the past several years, nearly twenty GE executives have been lured away to run other companies.

In fact, I sometimes think Jack Welch must have been a firefighter in another life. Because leadership has always been one of the key factors in the FDNY's success, we make a conscious effort to encourage our people to step up and embrace the leader's role. One way we accomplish this is by mentoring younger firefighters who show leadership potential, encouraging them to take the officer's test, and helping them study. We also rely on a strong network of unofficial leaders in the FDNY, people who aren't measured by rank or title but by experience, respect, and dedication.

To cultivate leadership in others is essentially to be a teacher, which means the whole process does indeed begin with you. You set the standards for your people, so to encourage leadership in others, you need to consistently model the kinds of values and attitudes you want your people to adopt. It also means you need to be in constant contact with them—talking, listening, and teaching them to unleash their leadership power and to take responsibility for their own performance.

In the beginning of this chapter I introduced you to the triangle of fire: fuel, heat, and oxygen. In the same way that you need these three ingredients if you want to start a fire, you need the three commitments if you want to fire up your leadership. And just as we extinguish fires by using water to turn heat into steam, or foam to seal off the fire from its oxygen supply, you disrupt your own leadership chain reaction by ignoring reality, neglecting your assets (your people), and smothering others' leadership potential. In the next chapter, which focuses on you, the leader, we'll begin to see more clearly and also in a more practical way how the three commitments interact to produce amazing results.

Straight from the Chief

Together, the three commitments make great leadership possible by supporting the strategies and disciplines that help you achieve your organization's goals. The commitments are uncovering reality (or as I like to call it, following the smoke), treating your people as assets, and developing leaders at all levels.

- To follow the smoke, you need to be out there all the time, gathering information from all kinds of sources, both quantitative and qualitative. You've got to be prepared to find and follow the smoke in yourself, your organization, and your industry if you hope to be effective.
- Your people are your true assets—they're the ones who make things happen, who get the job done. Make sure you give them the tools—and the leadership—they need to be effective.
- Every successful leader gets that way because he's backed by a core of subsidiary leaders who support his initiatives and goals. Spending time selecting and developing your support team is essential to becoming an out-in-front leader.

CHAPTER 3

Fueling the Leadership Fire

How do you take your leadership to the next level?

No one noticed the fire at first. No one was there to watch it flicker, then explode amidst the ready fuel of the warehouse. The first anyone even knew of its existence was when a night watchman smelled smoke at the intersection of Exchange and Pearl.

Initially, the fire was confined to a single five-story warehouse. Engine Company 1 soon arrived, but perhaps just a few moments too late. The fire was too much for their single stream and, spurred on by gale force winds, gorged itself on a succession of one, then two, then ten, then fifty buildings. Soon, most of New York's financial district was ablaze.

The alarm bell at City Hall brought the city's volunteer firemen rushing downtown, the teams of men straining at the ropes of their engines. They confronted the blaze, but this was December and it was cold; the hydrants froze, the hoses froze, and what didn't freeze was blown back in the firemen's faces by a scorching wind.

Finally the engines themselves began to seize up with the cold, so firemen dumped kegs of alcohol on them to keep the mechanisms free, and then poured brandy down their own boots to keep their toes from freezing together.

The fire was savaging the city. Buildings burned to cinders before anyone even knew they were on fire. A sperm oil warehouse exploded. Iron shutters and copper roofs melted. Ninety miles to the south, as Philadelphians watched the orange glow on the horizon, their city's firemen gathered their equipment and hurried north to New York.

Finally, a plan was conceived to blow up a building strategically located near the intersection of Broad Street and Exchange Place, to deprive the fire of its fuel and keep it south of Broad Street; if it jumped Broad Street, the entire city could be lost.

The plan, which would turn out to be successful only after several more buildings were demolished, was under way when the fire leaped onto the roof of the Tontine Coffee House, just north of Wall Street. Engine Company 13 was on hand to stop it, but their hoses couldn't reach the roof. Undaunted, the company's foreman directed his men to build a tower of rubble and discarded furniture, and placed his nozzle man at its peak. From there they laid water on the fire, and halted its northward advance. The Great Fire of 1835 had been defeated.

Fifteen years before that historic fire, the city's loose band of citizen firefighters had been exchanged for a force whose members, while still volunteers, were required to maintain higher degrees of discipline, technical prowess, and professionalism in order to deal with the multiplying demands of their growing city. But as the city doubled in population in the 1830s just prior to the Great Fire—from 125,000 to 270,000—and surged northward toward the farmland around Forty-second Street, the number of firefighters barely nudged, increasing from thirteen hundred to fifteen hundred. In relative terms, the number of New York City firefighters actually shrank, while their workload increased and also became more dangerous. New construction technologies were pushing buildings ever higher, yet at the same time, there was no such thing as fire safety, and building codes were completely unknown. Open flames proliferated in nineteenth-century Manhattan, and blazes, whipped up by the winds off the river, traveled so rapidly through the city that the broad east-west thoroughfares—Fourteenth Street, Twenty-third Street, Thirty-fourth Street, and Forty-second Street—were actually designed to act as firebreaks.

The Great Fire of 1835 was the first real test of this new department, and it passed with flying colors, despite the fact that the department was actually smaller than it had been fifteen years before. So what enabled this fledgling organization to meet that challenge? What was the secret weapon that enabled them to rise above so many obstacles?

In a word, leadership. Specifically, that of a veteran firefighter named James Gulick, who in 1831 assumed the top post of chief engineer, equivalent to today's chief of department. Under Gulick, the tiny department proved to be more than equal to the task of keeping the flames at bay, even as they threatened to consume all of Manhattan. The key to his success was his "first in, last out" leadership and the strong relationships he forged with the men serving under him. Because Gulick had won his men's respect and trust, he was able to enlist their support even when introducing unpopular changes, such as using teams of horses to pull the engines to fires, as opposed to the traditional practice of hauling them by hand. In addition, his management approach gave them the room to make their own decisions and get things done their way (like Engine Company 13's foreman ordering his men to build a tower out of rubble so that they could reach the fire and stop it from spreading uptown).

Gulick knew that leaders get things done through the relationships they make with their people. Or as Warren Bennis puts it in his book *On Becoming a Leader*: "Leaders deal with organizations and people, so it's natural that a leader would have to concern himself with the stuff of being human: values, commitments, convictions, passions."

Great leadership works through strong relationships, and relationships are reinforced by qualities such as communication, trust, credibility, transparency, and consistency of values and actions. Muddy personal values, poor self-confidence, difficulty communicating, and various other weaknesses make it impossible to form positive relationships with your people. This means you've got to face up to what's really going on inside you—yeah, I'm talking about the first commitment again—and identify and manage those leadership-limiting emotional triggers and weaknesses. *Insight* is one of leadership's essential qualities. And in this case, you need to develop some insight into who you are, because only by figuring out where you are as a leader can you get to where you need to be.

What follows is less a process, less a step-by-step leadership prescription, and more a set of ideas and thoughts about how to get to know yourself in a way that will help you become a more self-aware, confident, and purposeful leader. At the end of the day, you can hold only yourself responsible for the kind of leader you become.

UNCOVERING THE LEADER WITHIN

Getting some insight into your true self—your real values, goals, and motives—involves the same questioning and probing that we already discussed as part of following the smoke. The only difference is that in this case, the smoke you'll be following is your own. Once you figure out why you've made the choices you've made, or acted the way that you have, you'll be able to take control of yourself and manage your relationships with your people more effectively.

You've heard of Socrates, the ancient Greek teacher and philosopher? He taught by asking his students questions. Through the process of answering those questions, his students discovered the knowledge already inside of them. In this case, you need to be your own Socrates and learn to ask similar questions of yourself. Focus on key actions, events, and decisions in your past. Ask yourself: What really happened? Why? What did it do to me? What did it mean to me? Why did I make that choice? Was the outcome of that choice satisfying to me?

As you do this, stay alert for questions or topics that provoke emotions like fear or anxiety. These are often an indication that something is threatening your ideas or beliefs about something, and by retracing these emotions you can uncover the conflict and improve your self-awareness. A personal example of this that immediately comes to mind involves another firefighter, Billy McGinn. I first worked with Billy on 11 Truck, on the Lower East Side. This was before I made lieutenant. Now, Billy was sharp. God, how he was sharp. Even though he was only a probie at the time, he was a natural firefighter. He absorbed information like a supercomputer and was as brave and capable as anyone I've ever worked alongside.

Of course, I couldn't stand him. Who was this probie, to be doing all these things? I was so threatened by him, for months I wouldn't give him a break. Finally, the other guys began asking me what I had against him. It occurred to me that I had no idea why Billy bothered me the way he did. At that point, I became willing to try and find out. My willingness started me on the way to self-awareness. Gradually I came to understand why Billy made me feel so anxious—he was so good, he threatened my own ideas about myself—and by looking more closely at my emotional reactions to him, I discovered how to coexist peacefully with him and even learn from him. In fact, we became great friends, and later worked together in Squad 1 and 48 Engine, where he served as one of my lieutenants. Billy McGinn was with Squad 18 in the north tower on September 11 when it collapsed.

Successful and experienced leaders know that they must constantly pursue this kind of self-awareness in order to keep their edge. They understand that being blind to their emotional triggers or losing sight of their true values or goals can sabotage their leadership. This is why the best of them make time for reflection and meditation, to question and test the integrity of their decisions and actions. Clearly, developing self-awareness isn't something you can sandwich in between meetings.

You need to make time for it. I live in the suburbs, and the hour-long commute down to my Bronx firehouse means I have (at least) a sixty-minute block of time almost every day when I can engage in this kind of personal maintenance. I try to keep the cell phone off and always have in mind a few events that I think warrant a closer look: leadership moments in which I want to be certain of my decisions and my underlying thought processes.

Often, we don't understand what we know about ourselves until we articulate it somehow, get it out in the open. I'm sure you've discussed a problem with a friend only to find that just by talking it out you arrived at a solution. Or you've discovered that writing a report or a memo clarified the issues and suggested a possible course of action. It's the same with self-awareness. Once you get your values, ideas, and goals out in the open, you can evaluate them. One method of doing this is to discuss things with a trusted confidant, though I personally find that the act of writing is more effective. In fact, we use this same principle to help probies learn the finer points of the job. Every time they come to work they're expected to chronicle in a training notebook what they learn during the tour. The officers sign off on the notebooks and then test the probies on the content. We've found that for the probies, the act of writing down what they've learned, and then being challenged to understand it in connection to their existing store of knowledge, really facilitates learning and discovery.

After you've written down your thoughts, organize them into a personal statement that reflects your leadership vision. This might sound a little corny, but trust me: don't rush through it and don't blow it off. A personal vision statement provides you with a leadership code that you can lean on and even use as a teaching tool. Even if you write it down, file it away somewhere, and never look at it again, you'll find that the process will leave you with a sense of clarity and direction. Setting words to paper makes the ideas real, tangible, in a way that they couldn't be if left tangled in your mind with a thousand unrelated thoughts.

FIND YOUR ACHILLES' HEEL
BEFORE SOMEONE ELSE DOES

The same techniques that you used to get at key aspects of your self can also be applied to uncovering your strengths and weaknesses. Closely reexamining your long-held ideas about yourself, engaging in a personal Socratic dialogue, and examining your past will help you get a sense of your core capabilities. Also, by studying the gap between where you are and where you want to be, you can find out what you need to overcome or compensate for.

Another way to gather insights into your strengths and weaknesses is to recruit people whom you trust—your significant other, close friends, mentors, or even subordinates—and ask them to help you put together an assessment of your capabilities. These people can help identify your strengths, weaknesses, and blind spots—in fact, they've probably known about them for a long time. But before you ask them for help, be sure you're prepared to hear whatever they have to tell you. You don't have to accept their observations, but unless you want to damage a friendship, alienate a mentor, or piss off your spouse, be ready to thank them for their help no matter what unfortunate truths they expose.

I have a few friends, other officers, with whom I usually discuss these issues, but I also have my battalion aide. The aide is a firefighter who's assigned to the chief officer to serve as a kind of attaché, someone who helps execute decisions, manage personnel, and handle paperwork. But I also rely on my aide to let me know if I've screwed up somehow with my people. If I've come down too hard on someone (or not hard enough), I can rely on my aide to let me know: "Hey, Chief, that thing you did the other day . . . " Once I know about it, I can take care of it. I won't always agree that I've made a mistake, but thanks to my strong right hand, I know my chances of alienating my people or overlooking important information are minimized. He's got my back.

TURNING SELF-AWARENESS INTO A COMPETITIVE ADVANTAGE

So how can we use your newfound self-awareness to help you develop into a more effective leader? In this case, the word *develop* is the key. Self-awareness enables you to examine the gap between where you are now and where you want to be. Development, through learning and self-management, is how you're going to close that gap.

Learning can happen in all sorts of ways. You can learn by asking questions of your mentors, colleagues, and employees, and you can also learn simply by observing them. You can read books, such as this one. You can take courses, listen to tapes while you drive, and read magazines and newspapers. I also encourage you to expand your horizons by learning about things outside your industry too. For instance, I've read leadership books by politicians, professors, warriors, and CEOs, and I've found something in all of them that I could use. Leadership, after all, is a liberal art; it rests on a foundation formed by self-knowledge, wisdom, and a broad familiarity with the human condition and the range of activity of which humans are capable. I guarantee that for a leader, no learning is wasted.

One example of a world-class organization that believes in learning from leaders in other industries is the U.S. Marine Corps. In 1998, the marines partnered with the FDNY to learn about how their officers make decisions under pressure, communicate in an urban environment, and successfully lead small units in hazardous situations. The marine corps selected the FDNY because, as an article in the *Marine Corps Gazette* put it, "The firefighters' leadership, bravery and technical knowledge are tested on an everyday basis. When they show up to work, the call to fight their war is very real. They cannot hide behind rank, a desk, or e-mail."

Part of being open to learning is taking risks. You'd think risk wouldn't be a problem for firefighters, but we're like anyone else. Fear of failure keeps many of us from trying things a new way or attempting to acquire new skills, but all we do when we give in to this fear is entrench ourselves in mediocrity. All the firefighters I know who are really great, dynamic leaders have gone out of their way to put themselves in situations where it's guaranteed they're going to stumble at first. Maybe it's tackling some new procedure or piece of equipment, or transferring to a different branch of the FDNY, like rescue or hazmat. No matter what it is, the fact that they're pushing themselves and forcing themselves to learn new things means they're growing, improving. Don't look at your leadership career as a trial or a test but rather as an opportunity to grow and try new things.

But sometimes even a willingness to learn isn't enough. Sometimes our triggers lead to behavior or attitudes that need to stop *right now*. That's what self-management is about. Once you're aware of how your behavior or attitudes are undermining your leadership, you can transform your self-sabotaging actions into something more constructive. Think, for example, of the boss who, while holding a brainstorming meeting to generate ideas for an unhappy client, sneers at suggestions he doesn't like. He needs his staff if he's going to find a solution to the organization's problem, yet his behavior is killing his people's enthusiasm and sucking all the creative energy out of the room. If he realizes the harm he's causing, in time this bully could *learn* to communicate more effectively. But that could take a while. He needs to do something *right now,* and that something is to start monitoring his emotions. Then, the next time he feels the urge to lash out at his team, he can clamp down or *manage* that impulse and substitute a more productive response.

In the same way that you wrote down your thoughts and composed a vision statement, this time write down a list of all the weaknesses that are holding you back. Then identify a series of steps that will help you overcome or compensate for each weakness. You'll make it easier on yourself if you can also define an outcome for each step, so you'll know when you've accomplished it. For example, if your people seem to have trouble understanding what you want, then "Become a better communicator" is not a very helpful prescription. Instead, try something more concrete, like "Discuss this project with my people so I can confirm that they understand what I want from them." If you really want to give yourself every chance of success, assign dates of completion to each step so you have something to measure and motivate yourself with. Don't be too ambitious, however; a goal you can't meet will kill your motivation and is almost worse than no goal at all.

Most of what we've discussed in this chapter—awareness, managing your emotional triggers—could go under the heading of mental or emotional fitness, but there's also a physical dimension to leadership. When you're in good physical shape, you find that you can think more clearly, are more alert, and have increased stamina, all of which enables you to be more productive. Of course, in the FDNY, fitness has a more practical aspect. Even as a battalion chief, I'm still engaged in fire operations. I'm running up stairs, scaling ladders, and dodging flaming debris, all while wearing sixty pounds of firefighting gear. At the World Trade Center site we spent days clambering over several acres of razor-sharp obstacle course. But even if your job doesn't involve extreme situations, you can't lead out front if you're too stressed out and tired. And if you're not leading out front, you're not really leading.

Because leaders get their work done through their people, the more you understand and know about yourself as a person, the more you'll be able to deal successfully with others. Bossidy and Charan said as much when they identified a leader's key qualities: authenticity, self-awareness, and self-mastery—all of which flow from that first commitment, the commitment to reality. In the end, self-knowledge will give you the insight and wisdom to understand your people's values and goals, to help them discover and maximize their strengths while minimizing their weaknesses, and to enable them to perform effectively.

Now that you know who you really are, it's time to figure out who you really work for. In the next chapter, we'll explore how to uncover your organization's core values and goals and examine how the context in which you lead impacts your ability to be a successful leader.

Straight from the Chief

Getting to know yourself a little better will help you uncover and manage the emotional triggers that torpedo your leadership and sometimes lead to bullying, micromanaging, and other toxic behaviors. Once you take the steps to compensate for your weaknesses—through self-management or by learning new skills—you'll be better equipped to help your people do the same.

- Set aside time to reflect on past decisions, actions, and priorities. Ask yourself hard questions about how they relate to your motives and goals. Does your behavior reflect what you truly believe? Are your actions bringing you closer to your goals?
- Write down your values. Compose a leadership vision that sums up your beliefs about managing people. Then think about how well that vision matches your actions.
- Seek out friends, allies, and other leaders whom you trust, and ask them for constructive feedback on your management style. Have specific questions ready for them, particularly concerning areas where you suspect something might be wrong or where you seem to constantly have problems.

CHAPTER 4

Don't Waste Your Water on Smoke

How do you get your people to focus
on the things that matter?

It was Holy Saturday, the day before Easter, and I was standing on Arthur Avenue calculating what kind of fire would create so much furious black smoke. All along the front of the taxpayer—which is what we call a one-story commercial building divided into stores that share a common attic space, or cockloft—angry clouds rushed from every door and window.

That kind of smoke meant a good fire, a working fire, but it also meant by its volume and color that the interior of the taxpayer had probably gone from a contents fire to a structural fire. This marked the point at which the fire became robust enough to begin feeding on the building itself. But more than that, it also meant that the temperature inside the taxpayer was at least 572 degrees, the temperature at which most solid materials ignite, and very likely as hot as 1,000 degrees at the ceiling. To give you some context, the maximum survivable breathing temperature is 300 degrees, the term *survivable* being somewhat misleading. More than two minutes of respiration in such a superheated environment will seal your throat shut and kill you by asphyxiation. It's like drowning in fire.

We'd be using masks on this one.

The dense smoke was making it hard to determine the fire's origin. For anyone who's never been in a fire before, the most surprising thing about it is how little there is to see. The smoke is everywhere. It might be gray, brown, black, or tinted with green, depending on the fuel source and its temperature, but it's almost always dense, choking, and blinding. Entering a working fire is like being dropped into a tank of crude oil. I've been in fires where I can put my flashlight one inch from my mask and not catch a glimmer.

We deployed the men, who started forcing entry into the various stores, and soon came back to report fire in two areas. We were putting several thousand gallons of water on the fire when a captain reported to me that he'd found fire in the basement, heavy fire, really hot.

Fire in the basement is a very big deal. In 1966, a roaring inferno in the basement of the Wonder Drug on East Twenty-third Street ate through the beams supporting the pharmacy's floor, four inches of cement and one of masonry. The floor collapsed, dumping ten men into the very maw of the furnace. The resulting fireball killed two more firefighters. Twelve members of the FDNY lost their lives that day.

You never want your men working above an inferno like that, so we ordered everyone to back out from the ground floor of the taxpayer so we could redeploy to the basement. But we spend so much time teaching our people about the importance of the department's mission, and the values we cultivate result in such aggressive, goal-oriented behavior, that it's sometimes hard to get firefighters to fall back once they've engaged the enemy. Each of them feels personally responsible for executing the mission, and this is so deeply ingrained that it can actually work against them sometimes.

That was the case here. Looking back into the store where one of the attack lines had been stretched, I could see the firefighters silhouetted against a torrent of orange flame. And I saw the line actually inch *forward* a bit (despite my order to back out) as they continued to fight their way into the thick of the fire. Ironically, this was my old engine company, 48 Engine, where I'd been captain. So I guess you could say their gung ho attitude was somewhat my fault. This time, I stood on the hose and repeated my order to withdraw. They got the message.

I tell you this story to illustrate these firefighters' single-minded focus on the mission and their intense sense of personal responsibility. These are qualities every leader wants to see in his people, but the question is, how do you instill them in your folks?

The answers lie in your organization. Each has certain defining features that you need to be aware of in order to be an effective leader. The first, your organization's mission, keeps you focused on where the company wants to go and makes it possible for you to set objectives, create strategy, and allocate resources. The mission enables you to get the right things done. The second feature, your company's values, enables you to set standards and encourage behavior that will make your organization more effective as it pursues its mission. In this chapter, we're going to use insight to uncover these characteristics and discuss why they're important, how you can uncover them, and finally, how to use them to get results.

WHAT IS YOUR MISSION AND WHY DOES IT MATTER?

Successful leaders make things happen by defining their organization's mission and then using it to unify and focus their people's efforts. Practically speaking, your organization's mission should articulate your company's reason for being.

But while the whole idea of a mission is nothing new, most employees don't really understand why their organizations exist. If asked, I bet some would say that their companies exist to make a profit or to make money for their shareholders. Others might say that their organizations exist to make something or do something—for instance, Coca-Cola exists to make Coke, Ford Motor Company exists to make Fords, the FDNY exists to put out fires.

This confusion is the result of inattentive leadership. Yes, organizations do all this and more. But the real reason organizations exist is to provide their customers with value. Customers don't buy a product or a service, but a utility. For example, people don't buy cars: they buy freedom or status or even transportation. They purchase *value,* not products.

Most people, I think, would define the FDNY's mission as one of putting out fires. But if we were around only to suppress fires, that would mean that our customers, the people of the city of New York, place value only on extinguishing fire. The fact is, once you probe more deeply, you'll discover that what they really value is the *elimination* of fire. What our customers are really saying is this: If a fire happens to occur, then yes, please, knock it down—but we'd be so much happier if fires didn't start in the first place. So our mission isn't just fire suppression, but also fire prevention, which is why we spend so much time inspecting buildings, working with city planners and building code regulators, and teaching fire safety to New York City citizens. But on an even more fundamental level, our mission is to protect the people and property of New York City. In order to fulfill that mission and provide the value our clients seek, we also offer basic medical services, haz-mat operations, arson investigation, terrorism and disaster operations, and rescue operations in all kinds of environments, including high-angle, marine, aviation, subway, train, and automobile rescue; shootings and riots; wildfires; earthquakes; building collapse, and so on.

Since your customers define this value, your customers define your business. Organizations today need to ask themselves, Who is our customer? Only by figuring out exactly who their customer is and what they want can organizations fully grasp their mission. Organizations that ignore their customers and continue to define their mission by what they make won't be around for much longer.

PUTTING THE MISSION TO WORK

Organizations whose leaders haven't made the commitment to uncovering what their customers value have what's called an "inside-out" perspective. This means they're transfixed by the internal workings of their organization and define themselves by what they do, as opposed to what the customer values. In this situation, the organization is ruled by a warped kind of bureaucratic reality whereby internal processes, mechanisms, and politics become so important that they override the organization's original mission and purpose. Ultimately, the organization itself, and not its customers, becomes the reason for its own existence.

Interestingly enough, organizations like the FDNY are extraordinarily successful at remaining focused on their purpose and avoiding mission creep (the drift from an outside-in to an inside-out viewpoint). Without the discipline of a bottom line to focus the organization, it falls to our officer corps to provide discipline and direction. We accomplish this by teaching our people about the legacy of the FDNY. Battalion Chief Ed Schoales puts it like this: "The uniform is supposed to say something about you. You get it for nothing, but it comes with a history, so do the right thing when you're in it."

In addition to telling stories about what the organization means, we're constantly talking to our people about how the things we cover during our daily training and teaching sessions relate to the FDNY's overall objectives. We stay close to our customers through fire prevention outreach and inspection. All of these approaches enable us to stay focused on the things that matter—on serving our customers—and to concentrate our resources where they'll make the greatest positive impact.

So how can you use your organization's mission to become a better leader? Start by bringing that mission to life. As I mentioned earlier, the FDNY's mission is to protect the people and property of New York City. Obviously, that's a little vague. If that were the extent of our job description, we might have some problems. But by translating that mission into a set of specific goals, we not only make the mission coherent for our people but make it something that can actually be accomplished. Our goals revolve around things like response time, the kinds of emergencies we can handle, and our rate of success in suppressing fires and rescuing victims.

If your goals are well chosen and relate to your mission, they can help you discover new ways to deliver value to your clients, thereby giving you the edge on your competition. For example, during the bad old years in the city, during the 1970s and 1980s, people discovered that the FDNY tended to respond faster to emergency calls than the police department. So people began calling the fire department for all sorts of reasons. Over the phone they'd claim fire, but then when we arrived, we'd realize that someone just wanted five or six big guys around who knew how to handle themselves. Even though we'd never sought to provide this particular service, our goal of fast response enabled us to uncover other needs that did relate (in a roundabout way) to our mission of keeping citizens safe and secure.

Once you understand your organization's mission you can use it to guide your people and help them focus their efforts and allocate resources more effectively. By teaching them the principles of an outside-in perspective, you allow them to appreciate the full scope of the work being done in each area of the organization and how it contributes to the overall mission. Armed with this new perspective, employees will be less likely to indulge in turf wars or become blinded by narrowly defined self-interest. They'll be able to break out of the constraining viewpoints of their specific jobs and cooperate with one another to achieve meaningful results across the board.

WALK THROUGH FIRE FOR WHAT YOU BELIEVE

Just like other social organisms, such as families, tribes, and communities, organizations have distinct values that act as its social software. In other words, an organization's values, acknowledged or otherwise, govern what people perceive as acceptable behavior.

The FDNY recognized a long time ago how useful values can be in creating a high-performance organization. Because our mission is saving lives, we can legitimately lay claim to some pretty lofty values—things like love, bravery, and heroism—which are pretty awesome tools for raising people up out of their ordinary selves and inspiring them to do extraordinary things. However, we also rely on a fistful of operational, or practical, values to make sure our people embody productive attitudes and actions. For instance, we emphasize the value of physical and emotional fitness to make sure our people are able to withstand the burdens of such a physically grueling and emotionally draining job. We demonstrate values like focus and a constant awareness of one's environment, so our people are alert to what's happening around them—attacking a fire is no time to let your mind wander. Finally, we really impress upon everyone the value of brotherhood, of the bond between the men and women risking their lives, and how we're all responsible for one another and have to be able to depend on one another to come through a fire alive. We cultivate all these and more in order to support the FDNY's mission.

An insightful leader can accomplish great things by carefully defining and modeling a set of values that support the company's mission. Values can create habits and attitudes that contribute to higher performance, but only if they're enthusiastically supported and acted upon by the organization's leaders.

second takeaway? Don't be careless with values. I feel that
[...] n respond to an ethical crisis by issuing a new set of corporate [...] that usually have nothing to do with the organization's real
values. And nothing destroys their authority and credibility faster
than this kind of expediency. Employees want to respect their top people, but when they are subjected to this kind of thing they're left with
only two conclusions: either their leaders are cynical hypocrites who
don't care that the existing values of the organization are dysfunctional, or their leaders are totally oblivious to what's going on in their
own organizations. Neither conclusion generates any great confidence
in the leadership, which is why a quick-fix value statement is bound to
fail and will create more problems than it solves.

DEFINING YOUR BUSINESS TO DO BUSINESS

You uncover your organization's mission and values the same way you
uncovered your own: by following the smoke, confronting the underlying reality, scrutinizing past and present events, questioning and
probing (yourself as well as your colleagues, superiors, and customers),
and finally, by being willing to listen, even to what you don't want to
hear.

For example, almost everything I do in the fire department brings
me into contact with either our customers or our frontline employees.
I interact with citizens and firefighters every time I respond to a call or
conduct building inspections. This helps me stay in touch with what
our citizens want from the FDNY and also gather feedback from our
firefighters. It's pretty simple: if your organization's mission is shaped
by the value you bring to your customers, then you constantly need to
stay on top of what that value is, and the only way to accomplish that
is by staying as close to those customers as possible.

The irony here is that, as leaders move up through an organization, they get further and further away from their customers *and* their people. This means that by the time they're in a position to really change the organization's mission or values, they're so far removed that they may no longer understand what their customers want or what their people need. That's why it's important for leaders to go out and speak to their customers and frontline people as much as possible.

What can you do to stay close to your customers? Start by riding along with your salespeople, so you can see firsthand what your customers are saying about the organization. Interview suppliers and others who are part of your organization's value chain. And finally, use empathy and imagination to put yourself in your customers' shoes, and see your organization from their perspective.

Make an effort to connect with your people as well. Let them know you want to hear what they have to say. All of your frontline employees—whether they're firefighters or EMS technicians or salespeople or shipping specialists—interact with a customer, a partner, or a supplier every day. By spending time with your people, you can see for yourself whether your organization's values are inspiring productive behavior or are standing in the way of getting things done. Create processes that will encourage information to flow upward; fight the organizational gravity that makes information a one-way, top-to-bottom phenomenon. And if you have the authority, break down boundaries between groups and units so that information can flow into new areas and allow people to make fresh connections and discover new insights.

FIGHTING THE FIRE THAT HASN'T STARTED YET

After the 1993 World Trade Center bombing, Ray Downey, who was the battalion chief in charge of Special Operations Command (SOC), perceived that in the future the FDNY would be responding to an increasing number of terrorist incidents—not just bombings but bioterror, chemical-weapon, and even radiological attacks. Downey knew that the FDNY had to immediately begin developing a more advanced capability for dealing with those threats.

At that time, the FDNY had only one unit qualified to handle the unique emergencies that Downey foresaw: the SOC's haz-mat (hazardous materials) company, based in Queens. The term *haz-mat* covers a lot of ground: this company was formed in order to respond to everything from an anthrax attack to a fuel spill to a chemical plant fire. They have to go into a situation, figure out what kind of materials are involved, what sort of vapors are being emitted (Are they poisonous? Are they going to ignite?), and then they have to contain them. Investigation and mitigation. Haz-mat has A-level suits, B-level suits, onboard computers, and advanced analysis equipment. These guys have advanced degrees, master's degrees in scientific or technical fields; it's like having a rig of scientists, except that in this case doing their research means walking into an environment that's potentially more dangerous than any fire. Which was all great, except that there was only this one haz-mat company for a city whose future, as Downey saw it, was one of jackknifed fuel tankers, toxic fires, chemical spills, and terrorist attacks.

But Downey had a solution. There was already a unit within the SOC—Squad 1—that could be adapted to a haz-mat role. A squad is a unique, specially trained unit, similar to the elite rescue units, but instead of the large, distinctive rigs of rescue, squads use an engine apparatus. Like any engine company, they have a first-due area; if a fire happens in this area, they respond in an engine capacity, pulling hose, attacking the fire with internal and external streams, and so forth. Within a larger geographic area, however, they respond as a squad.

In their squad (as opposed to engine) capacity, these units are flexible and pack the punch of an engine, truck, or rescue force. They carry all the truck tools—extrication and forcible entry tools, ventilation and loss control equipment—as well as the equipment needed for high-angle, confined space, and collapse rescue.

So what Downey did was create six more squads, but this time he gave them haz-mat capabilities. Thanks to his prescience, the FDNY now has the ability to respond to multiple haz-mat emergencies and contain them until the main haz-mat company can arrive and take control of the incident. In the process of creating the new squads, Downey also gave the city a core of highly trained firefighters who could respond effectively to a variety of situations. Because of the cross-training they receive, squad and rescue guys can work practically anywhere, in any environment.

Unfortunately, a lot of organizations seem reluctant to face the changes in their industries. Demographic shifts, government regulation of some industries and deregulation of others, the effects of new technologies—all these represent some change in an organization's reality. And the test of an organization's long-term success will be how quickly it recognizes and responds to these changes.

Keep in mind that when we limit our exposure to information, or when information itself is scarce, our picture of reality suffers. We become oblivious to both opportunities and hazards. Trends become invisible. History disappears. It's really just two sides of the same coin: the first commitment is as much a commitment to gathering information, from as many sources and in as much volume as can constructively be used, as it is a commitment to facing the facts.

Companies need leaders who understand their environment and how the organization fits into it. Even if you're not the chief of department, you have a responsibility as a leader to know where the organization is going, how it's going to get there, and what obstacles and opportunities may lie ahead. At the very least, you need to understand your organization's mission and values so you can communicate them to your people and help them see how what they do is tied to what the organization does as a whole. If you don't understand your organization and can't communicate its meaning to your people, you can't possibly lead them. Neither of you would know where you're going or how to get there.

Finally, you need to remain committed to following the smoke and finding the fire—and not just once a year, but all the time. Keep developing yourself, opening yourself up to new ideas and information. Keep probing, questioning, and discovering. Stay focused on those things outside the organization that define its mission and shape its strategy—your customers and the business environment. It's particularly important that you keep this in mind, because in the remaining seven chapters we're going to focus on the inside—on your people, on what they value, and on how you can satisfy their values while leading them to new heights of performance and effectiveness.

Straight from the Chief

You can use your organization's mission and values to focus your people on doing the right things while keeping your organization on track. Also, once you know what's important about what your company does, you can see how changes in your industry will affect your organization, and prepare to meet those changes.

- Your mission flows from the value you offer your customers. If you really want to understand your mission, you need to understand the people you serve. Make it a priority to interact with a customer, or with someone who's constantly interacting with customers themselves, at least once a week.

- By making your organization's mission come to life, you'll be able to help your people focus on a common goal. You can make your mission come to life for your people by telling stories that illustrate key mission-oriented concepts or by using teaching approaches to reinforce the connection between what your people do and the bigger picture.

- Pay attention to your organization's values. And this doesn't mean just values like integrity or equal rights. By emphasizing the value of qualities like focus or pride in one's work, you can lead your people to higher levels of performance.

CHAPTER 5

Every Chief Needs a Radio, a White Helmet, and His People's Trust

How does trust help you get the most out of your people?

It was right around the time Lieutenant John Fox was deliberating over the cold cuts at the Key Food in Park Slope that New York City entered the twenty-first century. It wasn't a luncheon meat emergency that had called Fox to the deli aisle in his bunker gear, but a daily ritual of firehouse life: shopping for the next meal. In New York it's no big deal to spot a company of firefighters roaming the aisles of Pathmark or D'Agostino's alongside the other shoppers. But for their protective gear, and the apparatus idling outside in case of emergency, they might be just another family out running errands.

It was February 26, 1993. Before Fox could make up his mind between the ham and the roast beef, his chauffeur radioed him over the handie talkie. The Brooklyn dispatcher wanted Squad 1 at the World Trade Center. Outside, climbing up into the rig and taking the officer's traditional spot next to the chauffeur, Fox said that he wasn't expecting much from the call. But then, as they sped toward the Brooklyn Battery Tunnel, he switched over to the Manhattan frequencies. The frenzy of transmissions between the firefighters heading downtown and the FDNY dispatchers changed his mind. Then the calls started to come in. Third alarm. Fourth alarm. Two fifth alarms. We're going to be doing something over there, Fox decided.

As his rig came down West Street, Fox took in the scene: fire apparatuses were parked at ragged, hasty angles to one another; firefighters, their gear dragging at their bodies, trooped toward the gray soaring towers of the World Trade Center. It was a scene straight out of any of the city's great fires, except for one thing: no fire. The only trace Fox could find was a soft trickle of smoke that drifted from an underground parking garage.

Of course, what Fox couldn't know was that the first shot in a new global conflict had just been fired. Islamic extremists had exploded a rented Ryder van packed with a thousand pounds of fertilizer plus some hydrogen cylinders on the B-2 level of the Trade Center's parking garage. The blast knocked out seven stories of the garage. Before the day was out, six people would be dead, more than a thousand injured, and the stage set for an even greater catastrophe on that site eight years into the future.

The company fell in behind Fox as he headed over to the Vista hotel, where a command post had been established. Because of the squads' specialized nature, fire-ground commanders often use these units to plug holes in the attack or deal with unexpected emergencies. So Fox wasn't surprised when Deputy Chief Steven DeRosa saw him and said, "We're missing a man. Go downstairs." A missing firefighter is a high-priority situation. It's that bond again, the value of brotherhood. We can all picture one of our brother firefighters lying somewhere, trapped and possibly wounded, knowing we might be the only thing between him and a painful death. We want to do anything we can to rescue him, knowing he'd do the same for us.

In this situation, "downstairs" turned out to mean down into the parking garage. As Squad 1 descended into the earth beneath tower one, Fox suddenly understood what those two fifth alarms were all about. It was as if he'd taken a wrong turn and entered a war zone. Everything seemed to disappear into a smoky gloom. Water gushed from broken pipes. Wires and cables drooped from the shredded ceiling, sparking and snapping through the hot smoke. Cars were strewn across the floor of the garage. Covered in concrete dust, they almost looked abandoned; some were burning. Bright orange flames cradled and licked at the cars' crumpled bodies. There was no sign of the missing firefighter.

The missing firefighter's name was Kevin Shea; he was with Rescue 1. But he wasn't missing. At least, not from his perspective. He knew exactly where he was: lying on his back at the bottom of an enormous crater somewhere beneath New York's tallest building. His leg was injured, his radio was worthless, and all he could do was try and yell for help above the roar and crackle of the burning cars.

Fox and the rest of Squad 1 heard him, and made their way to the brink of the crater. Since Shea was too injured to climb out, someone would have to go get him. There was no discussion about who that would be. Lieutenant Fox was the officer. He would go. Since there was nothing to secure a rope to, the men from Squad 1, as well as those who had joined them from Ladder Companies 6 and 101, lowered Fox down until, finally, he hit the crater floor.

Fox looked around and spotted Shea. Above him, the upper levels that had been gouged by the explosion had begun to shed huge chunks of concrete, which pummeled the area around the two firefighters. Nearby cars had also begun to explode, spraying them with deafening blasts and shards of metal and glass. The officer crawled over to Shea and tried to shield him from the worst of it until the firefighters above them could organize a rescue.

I was the other lieutenant in Squad 1 at the time, and I always regretted not being there to be involved at the World Trade Center that day. Just my rotten luck to be off duty that day. As a firefighter, you hate to miss any opportunity to test yourself and see how you measure up. But even though I didn't get the chance to be there, I like to think I could have done as good a job as John. Which is not me being cocky. Part of what makes John so successful is something that I have too, and something that most leaders in the FDNY have: the trust of the people serving under us.

Trust is the only thing that makes leadership possible. In the FDNY, trust is what enables us to run into burning buildings when everyone else is running out of them. Trust in one another, and trust in our leaders. Our people believe that no matter what, their lieutenant, captain, or chief will do whatever it takes to beat back the enemy and bring them home alive. In a broader sense, trust brings objectives closer, makes people more effective, and allows your entire organization to rise above the everyday stress and anxiety that stifle performance. If your people don't trust you, then you have no influence over them beyond their paycheck, which is hardly the foundation of inspired leadership.

As a leader your job is to accomplish work and achieve goals through your people. So how does trust figure into that? Well, for instance, when your people don't trust you,

- They won't share their best ideas and innovations with you. Why? Any number of reasons. For example, they may think that you'll take credit for them or that you're too dull or bureaucracy-bound to recognize their value.
- They won't stick with you through tough times. When rumors of layoffs or financial difficulty are in the air, and your people don't trust you to give them the straight scoop, then you can count on your ablest people to desert you almost immediately, taking with them the talent and expertise you need to ride out the rough quarters.
- They won't open up to you and talk about the aspects of their character—their goals, strengths, weaknesses, and values—that

make it possible for you to get where they're coming from, and ultimately to lead them where you all need to go.

HOW TRUST SHIELDS YOUR PEOPLE FROM FEAR

Leaders in the FDNY serve as a kind of force field for their people, insulating them from excessive fear and stress. Whenever things start to get hairy, firefighters *know* that their officers will bust their ass to get them through the crisis safely. Because the men and women of the FDNY trust their leaders, they can focus all their energy on getting the job done, as opposed to sitting around paralyzed by the thought of all the things that might go wrong. Trust is an essential part of leading for performance, particularly performance under any kind of stress.

Trust plays a critical role in any organization. For example, the key to an organization's long-term success is its ability to change when necessary to keep itself competitive. And the only thing that makes it possible for people to tolerate the uncertainty, confusion, and pain that accompany any change—to give any change the benefit of the doubt—is trust. When your people begin to feel stressed, their confidence and faith in you actually act like a kind of force field that contains their fear and anxiety. Ronald Heifetz calls this force field of trust a "holding environment."

The key to using trust to boost people's performance under stress is to project an air of calm and control. As firefighters, we respond to all kinds of incidents, from gas leaks to plane crashes. The more intense the incident, the more we need to project a calm exterior. That's exactly what the chief officers—Hayden, Callan, and others—were doing as they supervised rescue operations from the lobby of tower one on the morning of September 11. You can see their command style in the documentary shot by the French film crew that happened to be there. Even as civilians were descending from the upper floors with horrible burns and bodies were slamming into the plaza outside, these leaders were very calm and measured as they discussed information, contingencies, and strategy. They knew that every firefighter who passed by the command post on the way to one of the tower stairwells would be looking to them for strength. Their calm, decisive manner gave those men and women the confidence to push their fears away and focus on their mission.

WHY YOU CAN'T *MAKE* TRUST

Unfortunately, while periods of stress highlight the need for trust, they don't really help you build it. Even if you act the hero during some kind of crisis—for instance, save someone's life, or work every weekend for a month to help your team make its numbers—it won't do much to build trust with your people. Trust comes from consistency. You have to work beforehand to develop it, but even then, what I've discovered is that you don't *create* trust. Trust comes from your people, not you. When your people see you at the head of the column, being the first one in, facing each danger alongside them, you simply create the conditions that make trust possible.

That's right: you can't make trust, you can only make trust possible. That's because trust is people's response to you when you act in ways that show them they'll benefit from following your lead. Basically, each person needs to believe that you have his or her best interests at heart—not that their interests are your only interests, but that you care about their needs and are committed to helping them satisfy those needs. Just as the key to business success is staying focused on what your customers value, the key to winning your people's trust is showing them that you're focused on what they value. Which brings up the question, what do your people value?

Not surprisingly, they value the same things everyone values: things like recognition, respect, and the chance to succeed and develop. For many firefighters, the way to achieve these things is by working at a busy firehouse. Busy means having lots of fires and emergencies, and fires and emergencies mean more chances to show what you're made of, to encounter new situations, and to hone new skills. Since not all houses see a lot of action, we show our commitment to our people by helping them transfer to busy houses. We also give our people development opportunities by rotating them through various fire-ground responsibilities. I might assign a guy to the roof on one call and then, on the next, have him doing interior searches or outside ventilation. By showing our people that we want to help them get where they want to go, we make it possible for them to trust us.

Trust happens because of two different things: competence and consistency. Competence leads to trust—people may respect you for your integrity and honesty, but they won't trust you to lead if you can't do your job. On the other hand, the intensity with which your people trust you comes from consistency. It's not enough to keep your word when you feel like it, or uphold your values sometimes, or be first through the door just now and again. You need to do it . . . well, maybe not always, but so often that people should be hard pressed to remember a time when you didn't. What makes this particularly tough is that no gesture or phrase is too small to escape their notice. Even tiny, routine actions—or inactions—can either encourage or poison a person's trust in you. Trust can drive you crazy that way: it takes years to build and moments to destroy.

HOW CAN YOU ENCOURAGE TRUST?

Any breakdown in trust can always be traced back to a leader's lack of commitment to following the smoke, especially as it relates to self-awareness. We've already talked about how leadership works through relationships. Well, trust is one of a handful of ingredients that make relationships possible. So self-awareness, along with an awareness of how others might see our actions, helps keep us alert to ways in which we might be short-circuiting our people's trust and undermining the relationships that help us lead.

All you need to do to create an environment where trust is possible is to let your people see how consistent you are in your decision making and how competent those decisions turn out to be. In other words, to build trust, leaders need to be transparent.

Daniel Goleman, Richard Boyatzis, and Annie McKee, in their book *Primal Leadership*, define transparency as "an authentic openness to others about one's feelings, beliefs and actions." Transparency is also another way of saying that leaders should be "first in, last out"—it's all about letting your people see you doing the things that matter. More specifically, transparency is making sure that your people have access to any decisions concerning their goals and the things they value. It's letting them see causes as well as effects, being open with them about standards, processes, and values, and treating everyone fairly. Your organization's promotion process, for example, should be completely transparent. Everyone should know what the standards are, and those standards should be fairly applied across the board.

The FDNY's system of leadership is founded on the principle of transparency. One way we accomplish this is through *the Test*. Administered once every four years, the Test is how firefighters qualify for the officer corps, and also how officers rise to higher positions. Every rank, all the way up to deputy chief, requires you to pass a different form of the Test.

Passing the Test is a full-time job. It takes immense dedication and discipline. The Test is usually only a hundred questions, but those hundred questions cover New York City building codes, structural collapse dangers, arson investigation, explosives, physics, engineeering, and management. You have to know the point at which every inflammable material ignites and building materials fail; you have to know reams of building and fire codes. You have to know firefighting tactics and strategy, command-and-control procedures, and management theory. Most guys study for years to have even a shot at passing the Test. It's like going to college all over again, except that if you fail a college exam, you have to take the course again; if you fail the Test, you have to take college over again. You have to study for another four years before you'll have a chance to retake it.

But what's really interesting about this Test is the effect it has on how our people react to their leaders. You've got to understand: everyone, from the newest probie to the most senior firefighter, knows about the Test. They know the breadth of the material it covers. They know how difficult it is to pass. And they know that only the most committed, enthusiastic, and competent men and women are going to qualify to become an officer.

Now I know that in other organizations, people can move up in rank for all kinds of reasons, none of which have a thing to do with eligibility. Maybe that freshly promoted manager's dad plays golf with the CEO, or that newly minted VP got lucky and rode a profitable business cycle for all it was worth, or the head of sales got promoted on the backs of her employees' hard work. This is the kind of thing that makes people suspicious of their leadership. You can't have credibility without clear standards. In the FDNY, on the other hand, the exams give us an indisputable measure of competence. The very act of qualifying for a leadership role confers credibility. That's why, for even the youngest lieutenant, the respect of the fifteen-year veterans she commands is hers to lose.

HOW DO YOU KNOW WHEN TRUST IS POSSIBLE?

To actually create an environment where trust is possible you need to work toward two different outcomes. Why two outcomes? Because it would be pretty damn annoying if I just told you to try and be "trustworthy." Instead, by achieving these two related outcomes, you'll find yourself hitting the trust target at the same time. The two outcomes are these:

1. Your employees aren't surprised when your actions and decisions inspire confidence in them.
2. You delegate as many tasks as possible to your people.

Outcome #1: Your Employees Aren't Surprised When Your Actions and Decisions Inspire Confidence in Them

When your people have confidence in your actions, and when this doesn't come as a shock to them, then you know you've made it possible for them to choose to trust you. When I'm leading an engine company into the heart of the inferno, this certainty is what I see in their eyes when I look back at them. But how do you get to this place?

One of the hardest things about trying to develop trust is recognizing which actions will support a trusting environment and which will wreck it. Using this first outcome, you can adjust your leadership trajectory simply by asking yourself, before you take action: Will this lead my people to have confidence in me? Is this action consistent with both my stated values and my past behavior?

As I hinted at earlier, trust begins with self-awareness. Use the methods we discussed in chapter 2, including setting aside time for self-exploration and recruiting others to give you feedback on your actions and attitudes, to get a sense of whether your people have all the info they need to choose trust. Ask yourself and those you've recruited questions such as

- Have I defined my standards and values for my people? If so, do I act in ways that measure up to those standards and values?
- Are my actions and decisions visible—do people know what I'm doing and why?
- Do I make an effort to include people in decisions that will impact them and their goals?
- Do I update them on these decisions and share with them the outcome?

What you discover when asking these questions will help you figure out how open (or transparent) you are with your people, and consequently, how likely it is that they have enough to go on when deciding whether or not to have confidence in you.

Make Sure Your People Know What to Expect from You

Now that you've established where you are in terms of your openness, you can develop objectives and strategies to help you improve. You can increase your people's confidence in you by consistently meeting their expectations, so your first objective should be to define and manage these expectations. Don't misunderstand: I'm not saying that you should spend all your time satisfying your employees' every whim. But the fact remains: since the only way to build confidence is to demonstrate that you can consistently meet expectations, you need to start by clarifying what those expectations are.

Begin defining expectations by recognizing your people's goals and being explicit about what you'll do to help achieve them. Explain to people exactly what they can expect from you in terms of helping them get what they want. If your commitments fall short of what they'd hoped for, then yes, they'll be disappointed. But as long as you do what you said you would, as long as you constantly meet their expectations, they won't lose confidence in you. Now obviously, if your commitment to them is less than what's perceived as the industry standard—if it's out of sync with what's usually offered by management—then they won't stick around long enough to see whether or not you can deliver consistently.

And don't forget that the whole point of setting expectations is then making good on those expectations. Which means you never speak in absolutes unless you have total control over the situation. When you say things like, "No one is going to be laid off," or, "You will definitely be promoted in the next year," but can't absolutely guarantee that those things will happen, you're setting yourself up for a trust disaster.

Also beware of the nasty flip side of this: the leader who waffles on everything can be trusted with nothing.

Make Sure Your People Know You're Up to the Job

Just communicating expectations, however, isn't enough. To create an atmosphere where trust is possible, leaders need to be competent as well as transparent. More to the point, you need to let your people see how good you are. Not surprisingly, they have a vested interest in how well you can do your job, since a more skilled and able leader will be more likely to help them achieve their goals than one who constantly brings down performance and effectiveness, infuriates top executives, fails to innovate, and so forth.

Once again, self-awareness plays a big role here. I'm sure there are plenty of leaders out there who are perfectly capable of getting the job done, but because of either unmanaged emotional triggers or runaway attitudes, they don't allow their people to watch them in action and see how good they are. What do I mean by emotional triggers and out-of-control attitudes? Well, take the boss who thinks all this stuff is just a bunch of wussy, touchy-feely crap. This guy may be willing to lead out front, but feels like he shouldn't have to. His attitude is, "Leadership means that leaders give orders and everyone else follows them. End of story." End of trust, too. Or take the manager who's so insecure about his communication skills that whenever he's called on to use them, he becomes defensive and withdrawn, shutting down transparency and killing trust.

Make Sure Your People Know You're the Best

One asset that can help you build trust is your reputation, particularly when you've just been promoted to a new position. A positive reputation can make people predisposed to have confidence in you. While reputations have a way of making the rounds all on their own—in the

FDNY, for instance, anytime a new officer is assigned to a firehouse, you can bet his men will know everything there is to know about him before he even takes command—you can maximize the power of a good reputation.

Get the most out of your glorious past by reaching out to influential allies—leaders either inside or outside your group that people trust—and telling them stories that showcase your ability to perform and deliver results for your people. Stories are a powerful way to spread information because once they can engage people's imagination, they are told and retold, taking on a life of their own. For your reputation-building stories, choose examples that clearly illustrate your ability not only to do your job but to help people accomplish their goals. When others hear these accounts of your successes, they'll be able to imagine you doing the same for them.

Of course, if you've already been around long enough for your reputation to be fairly well established, you'll need to rely on a different approach. To prove your competence to your people, include them in situations where they can see you perform. Pull them into the decision-making process, recruit them to work on special projects and new initiatives, and look for other opportunities where you can teach and work alongside them. By engaging them and letting them see that you're informed, insightful, smart, and decisive, and a leader who obviously wants to teach and develop her people (which is why you're giving them all these exciting opportunities), you create advocates who'll return to the group and vouch for your competence.

Not long after I made lieutenant, I was assigned to cover Rescue 1. "Covering" is like being a substitute teacher. When you're a covering officer, the department uses you to plug holes in firehouses all over the city. This means you're usually working tours in strange places where they don't know you and you don't know them. The good news about this particular assignment was that I had been a firefighter in

Rescue 3, so I was familiar with the tactics and tools that rescue uses. The bad news is I had less than ten years on the job. I was just a kid, and boy, I really looked it.

Rescue 1 is located in midtown Manhattan. Midtown means skyscrapers, and while it's not like I'd never encountered a high-rise fire before, Rescue 3 is in the Bronx. That's a different environment altogether, more residential and light commercial. High-rise fires definitely represent a unique set of challenges and dangers. Their very height cuts our available strategies in half. For example, tower ladders are the telescoping platforms that we use for exterior attacks. From these we can operate what's called a master stream. Master streams are the big guns of fire suppression, enabling us to drown a fire with five hundred gallons of water per minute, which is about 4,150 pounds of H_2O. However, since the tallest tower ladders in the department extend only ninety-five feet, any high-rise fire that occurs beyond that height means we have to rely on a far riskier *interior* attack strategy.

Probably the only beast more difficult to fight than a high-rise fire, in terms of sheer unpredictability and menace, would be a fully developed wildfire (something we'd really have to face only on Staten Island—and did in 1963). There are several reasons why a high-rise fire is so challenging. First, it's almost impossible to contain. The smoke and flames spread rapidly from floor to floor through the HVAC ducts as well as the utility shafts that run the height of the building. The open-floor layout of most office buildings means we have no way to physically contain a blaze: fires can flood through these spaces almost instantaneously, gobbling up cubicles. In addition, today's environmentally sealed skyscrapers also create what's called a stack effect. Produced by the building's air-conditioning and long, chimneylike stairwells and elevator shafts, the stack effect can draw smoke to a distant set of floors, where it cools and stratifies, forming a deadly cloud of toxic gas. And there are other dangers: open elevator shafts, concrete floors that buckle and spall at high temperatures, collapsing ceilings, and the grim possibility of becoming trapped by the fire.

My tour with Rescue 1 started slowly enough, but late that night a 10-75 came in, which means a working fire with at least four engine companies and three truck companies. Rescue always goes on a 10-75.

The fire was in a high-rise on West Fifty-ninth Street. It would later become known as the MTV fire, since it started in the offices of MTV. (Clever, huh?) When we arrived we found the engine companies already entangled with a monstrous blaze trying to break free from its floor of origin. They'd deployed two attack lines and were trying to force the fire back, but the best you could say was that they weren't losing the fight.

We got there just as the members of the engine company began running out of air. They were working off of thirty-minute bottles, but when you're at a fire, pushing your body to its limits, a thirty-minute supply runs out in about twelve. As they left the line to return to the street and resupply, Rescue 1 took their places. Here was my opportunity to show these men—very senior, experienced guys—that I knew what I was doing.

So I stepped in, took charge of the line, and made some good calls. We got the fire under control. But I never tried to order them around. I discussed the situation with them. I let them see why I was doing what I was doing. I also let them know that I'd had experience working in an engine company and handling the line. Ultimately, by being open with the men and letting them see how I worked, I was able to establish a basis for a short-term, situational trust. If I had come in and thrown my weight around, acted the part of the leader without establishing my competence, they still would have gotten the job done, but we would have been less effective and wouldn't have been as prepared for any unexpected events.

Outcome #2: You Delegate as Many Tasks as Possible to Your People

In addition to being a measure of your people's confidence in you, trust is also a matter of reciprocity. You need to trust your people if you want them to trust you. When managers squash their people's initiative and work style by imposing a micromanaging, one-size-fits-all approach to getting things done, they also make it impossible for their workers to trust them. Think about it: if your people were to place their faith in you when you obviously don't trust them to do their jobs without your constant oversight, then they would be going along with your low opinion of their abilities. And since most people don't like to think poorly of themselves, you can understand why employees never trust a micromanager or an overbearing, my-way-or-the-highway kind of boss.

Moreover, the most effective way to show your people that you trust them is to delegate to them. This is standard operating procedure in the FDNY. We don't hire people just so we can have the fun of doing their jobs for them. By pushing appropriate responsibilities down to your people, you show that you have confidence in them. By letting them tackle problems on their own, you demonstrate your belief in them. This sort of trust is inspiring, and your people will strive to be worthy of your faith in them by doing good work.

However, would-be leaders sometimes take delegation to mean something else. They seem to think it means inventing useless busy work for their people, setting them up for failure by giving them objectives that are impossible to achieve or pushing down only administrative or rote tasks. Wrong! True delegation means analyzing which decisions or projects can be handled effectively by which people, deciding who will benefit the most from the opportunity, and then supporting that person as she executes her new responsibilities. And remember, in addition to creating a kind of trust loop, delegation is also a way of forcing yourself to give away the superfluous tasks that distract you from your core leadership responsibilities.

Though we'll take a closer look at the nuts and bolts of delegation later in the book, I want to touch on a few things you need to keep in mind when pushing responsibility down to your people. Failure has never been much of a confidence builder, so remember that delegating won't help you build trust if you don't first make sure your people are prepared to succeed. There's a saying in the FDNY: "Lack of inspection leads to mediocrity." It basically means that you need to be checking in with your people, not to micromanage or to make sure they're doing it your way, but to see if they have questions, to correct mistakes on the spot, and to coach them through the rough parts. You should expect your people to make mistakes, so make it clear to them that they won't be punished for making the "right" mistakes. Instead, when they trip up while sincerely trying to help achieve the organization's mission, treat the failure as nothing more than an opportunity to spend some time working with an up-and-coming employee.

IF YOU LOSE YOUR PEOPLE'S TRUST, CAN YOU GET IT BACK?

Trust is a funny thing. When your people trust you, nothing gets them down and no goal is ever really out of reach. But the same person who inspires trust—in other words, the very source of all this strength—is also the only person who can ever really destroy it. If you're not paying attention, your hard-earned trust can quickly evaporate. For example, if you make expedient decisions rather than sticking to your principles, or don't do what you say you're going to do, or simply keep your people in the dark about things that concern them, you're destroying trust. However, if you can recognize this when it's happening, there's an approach you can use that will actually turn a failure of trust into a chance to renew and consolidate your people's confidence.

First, don't be afraid to change your mind if there's mounting evidence that you've made a mistake, such as a bad decision or an unfair action. Fess up to your error, explain what you're doing to correct the situation, and even ask for forgiveness, if necessary. Now, when I say ask for forgiveness, I'm not talking about whipping yourself bloody in front of your team every time you make a little mistake. But if you do something that affects someone negatively and suspect that it's going to have a harmful effect on your relationship with that person, then pull him aside and apologize. Sometimes I've made the mistake of correcting an officer in front of his men. When this happens (believe me, I try not to make a habit of it), I arrange for a few minutes with the officer later, in a casual setting, and tell him I'm sorry. I make it clear that while I meant what I said, I regret having said it where the men could hear.

If you've made a more strategic mistake, maybe by failing to foresee a change in the business environment or unwisely throwing more resources after a lost cause, then don't bother with an apology. This is a competence issue. But the only real incompetence in such a situation is the unwillingness to face reality, admit your mistake, and take action to correct it. If you can do those three things, you'll not only restore some of your lost trust, but you'll give people even more reason to have confidence in you. They know how valuable it is to have a leader confident enough in his own abilities to admit he's wrong.

Trust is easy to recognize, and hard to describe. When you've got it, anything is possible; when you don't, nothing seems to work. By describing these outcomes I've tried to define useful waypoints for a journey that every leader must travel. And like any good teacher, I've tried to explain to you the approaches I've used—transparency, setting and meeting expectations, demonstrating competence, reciprocity, and admitting mistakes—without insisting that these are the only approaches. If you know of other methods that will create an atmosphere of trust, then definitely use them and teach them to others in your organization. You'll earn their gratitude and, more important, their trust.

Straight from the Chief

Leadership runs on relationships, and to be useful, relationships need to be built on trust. When your people trust you, they're more engaged and productive. You can help trust happen by giving your people the information they need to feel good about putting their faith in you—that is, you need to give them some sign of your competence and consistency. A good place to do this is out in front, where they can see you.

- People need to have some experience with you in order to gather enough information to decide to trust you. Use existing processes like meetings or reviews as opportunities to build credibility. Seek out opportunities where your people will be able to see you doing great work.
- Make sure your people know what to expect from you; if you don't manage their expectations, you'll never be able to meet them. Also make sure your people know that you're great at what you do; leverage your reputation, as well as communicate any "war stories" that showcase your ability to deliver results.
- Resist the temptation to micromanage your people or do their work for them. By delegating to them, not only do you free up more time to focus on your leadership functions, but you also show your people that you trust them. This is a powerful gesture, and as long as they don't feel that you're simply dumping busy work on them, they'll work hard to show that they're worthy of your faith in them.

CHAPTER 6

Know Their Names Before You
Send Them into the Flames

How do you create strong connections with your people?

"As I raced through the stairwell, between the seventh floor and the sixth, I heard that noise again. That same sick, killing rumble. . . . There was no mistaking the roar, and as it quickly approached I knew what it meant. We all knew what it meant." For Richard Picciotto, commander of Battalion 11, and the other firefighters who had rushed into the north tower on September 11, this is what it was like when the world ended.

I wasn't able to get downtown until about an hour after the second collapse. I still remember the raw moment of my arrival at the command post at the corner of West and Vesey. I think all the coverage since has made us a little numb, but looking back I can still remember how the devastation stabbed me. The acres of fresh, smoking wreckage. The carcass of the Vista hotel in my foreground. The fires feeding off the remains of 3 and 6 World Trade Center.

A friend of mine, Captain Jay Jonas (now battalion chief), was with Ladder 6 that day, in Chinatown. Ladder 6 was one of the second-alarm units, and one of the first operating companies to arrive. Jay and his men were on the upper floors of the north tower, helping injured civilians, when the south tower collapsed. They weren't exactly sure what had happened—there was nothing to see out the windows but a blizzard of ash—but they knew it was something catastrophic. They were descending to the ground floor of the north tower when that building failed as well.

Jay and his five firefighters made up six of the fourteen people in stairway B (including Chief Picciotto) who had survived the collapse. Shortly after my arrival at Ground Zero, I heard Ladder 6 on my portable handie talkie. (That is, I heard Jay. We always refer to officers by their company or battalion.) I was surprised to hear from him, not because I hadn't expected him to survive, but because it hadn't occurred to me that maybe my friend Jay was working on that particular day. I don't know why, but I hadn't started thinking about all the people I knew who weren't coming home that night, even though I had dozens of friends down there.

So here we are, Jay and I, talking to each other on the radio, and I'm trying to determine where he is and what his condition is and what the problem is. And of course we quickly find out that he and his company and some other people are trapped inside the debris pile. Jay was so calm, so controlled, you would've thought he was calling from his front porch. It was hard to believe that he was entombed inside the wreck of a 110-story skyscraper. Other officers who knew Jay and could also hear him over the radio would jump in on the conversation, and at one point someone asked, "Jay, where exactly are you?" And Jay replied, "I'm in the B stairway in the north tower. Go in the front doors, and make a left. It's the first door on your right."

Of course, what Jay didn't know is that there was no longer a north tower, or front doors, or stairway B, or anything other than a smoking mountain of debris. So while this story is kind of funny and tragic at the same time, it's also a good example of how important it is to have a common frame of reference when communicating with people, a shared starting point. Often, what a leader says and what his people hear are two different things, mainly because each of them sees the same things from a different perspective. This is something all of us leaders need to address, since effective, two-way communication is essential to forming useful relationships with your people.

YOU NEED TO KNOW WHO YOUR PEOPLE ARE BEFORE YOU CAN TELL THEM WHAT TO DO

In their book *First, Break All the Rules*, Marcus Buckingham and Curt Coffman define healthy companies as those where managers have developed strong bonds with their employees. This shouldn't come as a surprise. You need to establish solid connections with your people in order to motivate them to create value and do good work.

But why exactly do you need to connect with your employees in order to lead them? That probably doesn't sound like the kind of hard-nosed leadership you imagine when you think of firefighters. But even during the heyday of time-and-motion studies and the Industrial Revolution, firefighters were more like today's knowledge workers than like the factory laborers who were plugged into assembly lines and other process-oriented productivity innovations. To fight fires and deal with other extraordinary emergencies, people were needed who brought their own special strengths and approaches to the work. And to make such people effective in deploying their individual skills, employers have to get to know them as individuals.

Today, most industries have moved away from work that lends itself to an assembly-line, all-workers-are-interchangeable approach, and offer products or services that rely more on their employees' specific strengths and abilities. That's why the goal of leaders and managers today is to "make productive *the specific strengths and knowledge* of each individual." This fresh outlook, combined with studies showing that different people need to be managed in different ways, makes for quite a change from the old days. Instead of one-size-fits-all management, you need to develop a relationship with each person that lets you understand his or her individual strengths, weaknesses, style of working, and motives, and then leverage that understanding to produce effective work.

WHY A WORKING RADIO IS WORTH MORE THAN TWENTY THOUSAND GALLONS OF WATER

To develop connections with your people, however, you first need to be able to communicate with them. In fact, communication is such an essential part of leadership in the FDNY that the speaking trumpet (basically a crude bullhorn) that foremen used to shout instructions to their firefighters in the early days is now (in the form of a gold insignia) used to indicate an officer's rank.

Luckily, we've made some progress, communication-wise, since the days of the speaking trumpet. We've discovered something essential about communication, and that is: communication is all about perception. In fact, Drucker uses the question "If a tree falls in the forest and no one is there to hear it, does it make a sound?" to explain what that means. He argues that since no one is there to receive the sound waves created by the falling tree, no sound—for all intents and purposes—is created. His conclusion? Communication happens only when someone receives a message. And since every time we receive a message we process it in terms of our own prejudices, concerns, and assumptions, we tend to filter all communications through our own little worldview.

What this means for us as leaders is that probably only 50 percent of what we're trying to get across is really understood by our people. One of the most common frustrations I've heard from leaders is that their people "just don't do what we tell them to do." However, given what we now know about the nature of communication, it's more likely that the problem lies with the leaders themselves. All of us make the mistake of focusing only on what we're saying, and not on what our people may be hearing.

Take, for example, the manager who calls his team together to announce that because of changes in the business environment, the company will need to go through some changes in order to serve its customers better. Now, having all been employees at some point in our lives, we can appreciate how people might take this to mean that layoffs are on the way. So instead of returning to work reenergized, champing at the bit to come up with new ideas that will help the organization stay competitive, the demoralized team returns to their desks and starts sending out résumés. This might have been avoided if the leader had taken the time to try and understand how his employees' concerns might shape their perception of his message. The moral is, if you want to be sure that your messages are getting through intact, then you need to frame the message in terms that your people will understand.

You can find the raw material for this shared frame of reference in your people's individual goals. For example, I'd approach a firefighter who I knew was trying to study for the Test differently than I would one whose goal was simply to do a great job and then go home to his wife and kids. By talking with them about how their own goals relate to the organization's goals, I can develop a useful frame of reference for communicating with each of them. But I wouldn't be able to accomplish this if I isolated myself at the top of the org chart, throwing presentations, memos, and e-mails down at my people. Instead, I need to get down to their level so I can appreciate how the world looks from their point of view.

Ultimately, establishing a common frame of reference requires a leadership communication style based on self-awareness, insight, candid dialogue, focused listening, empathy, and of course, trust. In other words, it takes a lot of hard work and perseverance.

In this chapter I discuss three outcomes that will guide you in communicating and forging connections with your people. You'll know that you're well on your way to making these connections happen when

- Your people feel that you understand their personal goals and motives, and sincerely want to help them achieve those goals.
- Your people know what's going on in the organization, they understand its mission and values, and most important, they see how their own goals are linked to the organization's goals.
- Your people feel that they have a good work environment, and it enables them to do their best work.

As we look over each outcome, we'll examine several methods and approaches that will not only make you a more effective communicator, but also help you develop your people and put them in a position to do great work.

Outcome #1: Your People Feel That You Understand Their Goals and Sincerely Want to Help Them Achieve Them

I'll start by stating the obvious: no one does anything for nothing. In fact, I think the line "What's in it for me?" is etched into our DNA. But there's nothing particularly shocking about that. People act, and they act most energetically and purposefully, when they feel like they're working toward their own objectives.

At this point, someone always mentions the paycheck. Don't talk to me about the paycheck. I've got guys risking their lives, running into infernos for strangers—and not just for clean-behind-the-ears Upper West Side types, but drug addicts, criminals, the good, the bad, and the ugly—for a civil-service salary. Clearly, it's more than cash that motivates people to work.

Once you understand what your people really want, you can show them how what they want intersects with what the organization wants. Linking their own aspirations with the larger objectives of the company aligns all their effort, enthusiasm, and energy—and their "What's in it for me?"—with what your organization's trying to accomplish. This is the key to the high-performing organization. The trick, of course, is finding out what those goals really are. You can't simply order your people to tell you. And you can't have them fill out a form. Only by connecting with your people can you uncover their true goals and aspirations.

So how do you uncover those goals? It's pretty simple, really. All you have to do is ask. However, there's no point in asking people unless you've already begun building a relationship with them. Only in a context of trust and caring will people confide to you their true goals and motives. Otherwise, they'll just feed you what they think you want to hear.

This is not to say that you'll build relationships with your people the same way that you would with anyone else. While the way you go about developing the connection itself is the same—you do it by asking open-ended questions, sharing information, and listening to what other people have to say—instead of asking them exclusively about their personal life or their childhood, you'll ask them about things that will help you lead them more effectively. For example, you might ask questions like

- How do you like to receive criticism or feedback?
- How do you like to receive praise?
- Do you appreciate when I drop by to check in, or would you rather schedule a time when we can meet and chat about how your work is going?
- How do you think you learn best? Is it by experimenting and finding your own way, or by watching others and being coached through the process?

Finally, here's a little tip that's worth remembering: try not to use the first person when speaking to your people. When you constantly use "I" to start a sentence, it draws attention to you, and makes you sound insincere. Not too helpful if you're trying to establish a connection with them.

Create Common Ground, Then Communicate

The more you can find out about how a person looks at the world, the better you'll be able to communicate with him. Buckingham and Coffman observed that "a great manager must get to know his employees." This is exactly what we do in the FDNY, and describes in a nutshell what you should be doing as well: consistently engaging your employees in conversations, asking them questions, and listening carefully to their answers.

When I was a lieutenant, and then, later, a captain, I had plenty of chances to get to know the guys under my command. After all, on any given tour I had only the five guys of my company to worry about, so I really got to work with each of them and know them as individuals. But now, as a battalion commander, it's not quite so easy.

Even with more than a hundred people under my command, the department feels (and I agree) that I can't be an effective leader unless I'm able to create some kind of connection with these people individually. That's why a large part of my job consists of visiting the various companies under our command, either formally or informally, as often as possible. I observe training, go over new procedures or regulations, and literally sit down with the men to discuss recent operations or hear their concerns about issues ranging from budget cuts to promotional exams. Some people call this "leadership by walking around." It accomplishes several very valuable things: it enables us to get to know the people working for us, which is particularly important nowadays with so many new faces in the department; it lets our people know that we care about them and what they have to say; and it also allows us to see how things are going in the various firehouses.

The first step you should take if you want to adopt a similar approach is to decide to really care about your people and their objectives. And if you're not sure that you really do, then ask yourself this question: Do I care about myself and my career? If the answer is yes, then you care about your people, too; after all, they are the ones who will *make* your career.

So far, I haven't mentioned the art of listening, but obviously, if you don't listen to your people, you can't collect the information you need in order to build relationships with them or uncover their goals. And by listening, I don't just mean waiting for them to finish talking. I mean really focusing on what they have to say.

Focused listening is nothing more than listening with *purpose*. Plan ahead—not weeks ahead, but a few moments before starting up a conversation with someone—and figure out what you want from the encounter. Think of an objective you'd like to achieve by the time you walk away. By keeping in mind what you want to accomplish—let's say, for example, that you want to find out how they like to receive feedback—you keep yourself focused on what the other person is saying. There's really no magic formula. Listening is a function of self-interest. People pay attention to things that relate to their own needs, so if you want to listen well, just figure out why you're listening.

Listening is so highly prized within our organization that some leaders are respected for their ability to listen as much as for their command presence or decisiveness in tight situations. Our former chief of department, Dan Nigro, is one of those men. I can think of several times when Nigro's willingness to listen to his people or put their observations or expertise to use has enabled us to succeed in our mission, but for me the incident that epitomizes his value as a leader who knows how to listen happened early on the morning of September 11. Even amidst the chaos of that morning, he took a few precious moments hearing the fears of and comforting a firefighter who was worried about his wife, who worked on the ninety-second floor of the south tower. I carry with me, as a lesson and an inspiration, the image of Nigro pausing in the midst of all that chaos and just listening to the young man's worries.

Now, what I haven't touched on yet is the very real possibility that your people would rather endure slow torture than risk having a genuine conversation with you. Many people think of their boss as someone who gives them a lot of work and then yells at them when they don't get it done quickly enough. If you do happen to make your people nervous, it will be pretty obvious, especially the first few times you try to engage them in conversation. My advice? Don't worry about it, and don't make things worse by trying to be too buddy-buddy too fast. Just be patient and keep doing what you're doing; they'll come around.

Your People Need to Know You've Got Their Back

So far, I've talked a lot about how you can forge connections with your people, but that's only part of your goal. You also want to make sure that your people feel you're committed to helping them be successful. Practically speaking, this might mean that you make sure an employee gets access to specific developmental opportunities, such as the chance to work on a project that will give her some leadership experience. Or it might mean that you give her frequent and honest feedback, or that you take the time to coach her past a weakness that's been holding her back. My point is that although the outcome you're looking for—a scenario where each person feels that you want to help her achieve her goals—may sound like it requires you to be a full-time personal coach, it really involves nothing more than creating a specific kind of trust.

What you're not doing is promising someone that you, personally, will make sure she achieves her goals. You're not committing yourself to a particular *outcome*, you're just committing yourself to a *process*. Once you've uncovered her goals, explain what you'll do to support her in reaching those goals. In other words, set expectations. Once you show that you'll consistently meet these expectations, your people will have the evidence they need to make the decision to trust you, thus deepening your connection with them.

I know we've already covered a lot of ground in this chapter, so let's quickly recap what we've learned so far: first, that in order to uncover your people's motives and goals you need to develop a relationship with them; second, that relationships flourish only where there is good communication and a shared frame of reference; and third, that developing this level of communication takes open dialogue, sincere questions, and focused listening. Now, in the next section, I'm going to show you why all this is useful to you as a leader, because while it may seem like I'm just trying to get you to be a nice-guy boss, what I'm really doing is getting you ready to solve an age-old management riddle: how to get your people to do the right things.

Outcome #2: Your People Understand Your Organization's Mission and Values, as Well as How Their Own Goals Are Linked to the Organization's Goals

In this section you'll learn how, by making your organization's mission and objectives tangible to your people, you can draw on your relationship with them to align their goals—and their efforts—with those of the organization.

By sharing your organization's objectives with your people you create a point of reference that you can return to in future conversations. This common frame of reference is not only what makes communication work, but also what allows your people to do things like evaluate their own performance, identify their own strengths and weaknesses, and come up with innovative new ideas to help the organization. Finally, a company-wide awareness of objectives enables you to speed the acceptance of new initiatives, alert your people to shifts in the business environment, and manage change more effectively.

What Should I Communicate to My People?

The point of sitting down with your folks and explaining the basic components of your organization to them isn't so they can parrot back to you some corporate pledge of allegiance. The only reason for teaching this stuff is so that your people can use it to keep themselves focused *out*, on the customer's needs.

Just think of how powerful your organization will become when all your employees start from the same assumptions about what they're trying to accomplish as a company. Suddenly, the people in legal will understand that their job is not to serve the goals of the legal department, but the goals of the customer. The IT department will realize that they exist not to buy cool software or systems, but to act in ways that ultimately create value for clients. We've always had this kind of unified focus in the FDNY, but then again, it's hard to ignore that big fire that's threatening to storm through a whole block.

Just the same, I feel we've always benefited from the outside-in perspective that comes from teaching our people about their organization's purpose. Understanding this purpose and mission is what allows people to make their work compatible with others' work in the organization and brings them together around a common vision. In addition, this information makes it possible for them to be innovative, take initiative, and be self-directed in their work.

That's why it's important that you take the time to discuss these things with your people. And for crying out loud, you can't leave it to Human Resources. Even though probies get a dose of the FDNY mission and values out at the academy on Randall's Island—affectionately referred to as the Rock—as soon as they're assigned to a firehouse the company officer and top whip focus on teaching them what it really means to be a New York City firefighter. And I guarantee you, the first thing they focus on is the mission. Everyone joins the FDNY because he wants to knock down fires. So it's our job as leaders to show the new hires that we're not here only to fight fires. By using the job itself as a teaching tool—every fire inspection, EMS run, and emergency incident is a lesson—we help them understand that the organization's objectives encompass much more than just fire suppression.

Your organization's fundamentals offer you a real opportunity to focus and orient your people's efforts, but only if you spend time teaching them one-on-one what these ideas have to do with their jobs. If you don't engage employees in a discussion about these basic concepts—if you instead disseminate them via company-wide e-mail or memo—then you're not only wasting your time, but squandering the power of these principles.

How Do You Communicate These Things to Your People?

What we sometimes lose track of in the day-to-day is that as leaders our job is really to take people beyond themselves. For example, everything we do is part of our drive to make people more productive, effective, or useful than they already are, to help them live up to their potential. In this sense, leaders have a lot in common with teachers. And just like teachers, we communicate best by showing, not telling. We need to do less commanding and more coaching, if we want to get results. Here are a few simple guidelines to help you make your messages, starting with your organization's mission and values, stick:

- **Know your topic.** As with all forms of communication, you've got to know what you want to accomplish before you start. Make sure you know exactly what you want to communicate, and use that to guide your discussions with your people. And make sure you can explain something to yourself before trying to explain it to others.

- **Keep it simple.** Don't digress, don't jump ahead, and don't use terminology or phrases that people may not understand. Your goal is to educate, not to impress or overwhelm with the depth and breadth of your knowledge. Stay focused on the information you're trying to convey. Keep your tone pleasant and respectful.

· **Seek constant feedback and encourage dialogue.** This is where teaching really happens. As you approach key points in your explanation, pause and ask questions about what you've just covered. The answers you get will not only help you gauge people's comprehension and give you a chance to adjust your approach, but also spur new thoughts, discoveries, and perspectives. (In fact, this works even if you're just giving orders. If you want to make sure someone heard you and is going to do what you asked, have them repeat your instructions back to you. We always do this in the department to avoid any potentially deadly misunderstandings on the fire ground.)

Teaching is mainly about asking provocative questions and then supporting people as they work through the answers. Teaching creates a dynamic relationship, one in which teacher and student are constantly exchanging ideas and insights, as well as roles. In the end, you'll probably learn as much from your people as they do from you.

But incorporating a teaching approach into your leadership communications will get you only so far. The other piece of the puzzle is finding the right time to teach your people. After all, you're running a business, not a university. Not many leaders are fortunate enough to work for organizations that set aside time for training and development, as they do in the FDNY. Firefighters have the opportunity to attend thirteen different training schools, from Building Collapse Training to Technical Rescue School. As part of every tour, we spend at least an hour drilling, training, and teaching. And in addition to that hour of formal teaching, I probably spend about 50 percent of every day coaching and developing people.

Make the Job into Your Classroom

How do you do this? By using something I call "opportunistic education," and it's actually pretty easy. Simply watch for and take advantage of the teaching moments handed to you by the everyday routine of your organization. Things like meetings, employee reviews, the budgeting cycle, and the announcement of new initiatives are all standard organizational processes that you can turn into opportunities to renew your message.

Another part of opportunistic teaching is using examples—and these can be specific to your industry or simply best practices or cautionary tales from other organizations—to give whatever you're teaching some real-world impact. As a company officer, I was responsible for training my company in everything from maneuvers and tactics to learning some new piece of equipment, as well as for enhancing team coordination. And so I was always thinking about ways to make what I taught more memorable. I started keeping a notepad with me so I could jot down things I picked up from books or magazines that were applicable to the material I was covering at the time. I used the Internet and the library to track down articles that related to the concepts I was teaching. I discovered videos that I thought would help my people absorb the info I was trying to convey.

And even though I'm no longer a company commander, I still use opportunistic teaching with the people in my battalion. For example, whenever I read an article that I feel my officers or firefighters could benefit from (an article about anything from decision making to new building techniques), I'll make copies and take them to the various firehouses I work with. I hand them out and talk about them with my people. The articles never fail to spark some useful discussion, and as a result I almost always discover new ways of looking at familiar problems. In fact, I find the most valuable thing about this approach is the way it draws people into a conversation or focuses them on a particular topic. The new ideas and insights that are shared as a result of these conversations are the nourishment that any organization needs in order to grow.

Good teachers often tell stories in order to help their messages stick. Good leaders are no different. For example, Abraham Lincoln knew that he could use stories to get his point across more powerfully than any argument or sober presentation of the facts. "I often avoid a laborious explanation on my part by a short story that illustrates my point of view," he explained.

When a leader uses stories to convey his organization's mission and values, he's really answering such profound questions as Who am I? Who are we? Where are we going? What is our purpose? And while few of us have Lincoln's rich supply of anecdotes and tall tales, the inspiration for your own stories is all around you. If you want to teach people about your organization's mission, then tell them the story of how the company began. What did its founders want to accomplish? What need did they see in the market? Or tell the story of one of your customers. Why did they come to your organization? What value did they find there?

The FDNY has always used stories—and it has used them very effectively—to preserve and perpetuate its core values and mission. The moment probies show up at their assigned firehouses for their first day on the job, they're inducted into the culture of the department through the stories and legends told to them by the veterans. We tell them about Captain Patrick "Paddy" Brown and his legendary acts of bravery. We talk about Tom Neary, who approached every fire as if it had just insulted his mother: he used to do things like rip the doors off apartments and use them as a shield while he charged through the flames. Stories about Brown and Neary describe some of the qualities that firefighters should have, the values they should embody. But sometimes our stories have a more practical aspect. For example, we often describe operations where guys were particularly sharp, as well as operations where guys made mistakes. In both cases, we do this to illustrate basic concepts or techniques that we want firefighters to adopt in their own approach to the job.

One of my favorite stories told in the firehouse illustrates the significance of the FDNY's symbol, the Maltese Cross—you can find it on the cover of this book—but also speaks to our values of brotherhood and sacrifice. The story dates all the way back to the Crusades. The Knights of Saint John, one of the groups of Crusaders who invaded the Holy Land, had laid siege to a Saracen city. Unbeknownst to the knights, the Saracens had developed a new weapon: an inflammable liquid they called naptha. Placing the naptha in glass containers, the Saracens bombarded the knights with it until they were soaked with it, and then hurled torches at them. Hundreds of knights were instantly consumed in a furious blaze, while hundreds more—history's first firefighters—rushed into the burning chaos to save them. The knights later settled on the island of Malta and their emblem became known as the Maltese Cross. For us, both the symbol and the story it tells are ever-present reminders of our mission.

How to Link People's Motives and Goals to the Organization's Mission and Objectives

The key to linking your employees' goals with your organization's objectives lies in your ability to bring together all the methods we've discussed so far. That's because what you're trying to achieve here— convincing your people that the best way to get what they want is by working toward what the organization wants—goes against everything they've learned so far in our labor-versus-management culture. Only if you give them the info they need to trust you will your people be able to believe that you have a sincere interest in helping them achieve their goals. And only a combination of teaching methods and storytelling will help them understand how their goals and their organization's goals are linked. And because you'll probably need to periodically renew that link in order to make it stick, stay alert and watch for teaching opportunities you can use to hammer home its relevance to your people.

In the FDNY, we're constantly looking for chances to show our people how their personal objectives dovetail with the organization's goals. Although the FDNY's mission is to save the lives and property of New York's citizens, most people don't really join the department because they have their heart set on haz-mat operations, or providing first-response medical services and support. By and large, they join because they want to fight fires. Now, whenever I tell people this, I always get some strange looks. *You mean they actually want to fight fires? They want to risk their lives for strangers?* And the answer is always yes, absolutely. Why else would someone become a firefighter? Unlike in the early days, when firemen were local heroes and role models, it's not a glamorous profession. It won't make you rich, and it probably won't do much for your health. But it's meaningful work and it's exciting.

But while people join the department to knock down fires, that's not why the department exists. In fact, while much of our work is related in some way to fire suppression, we contribute to the organization's mission in a number of ways: by mastering new equipment or tactics, developing skills that will enable us to deal with new kinds of emergencies, providing medical support, and working with other city, state, and federal agencies to keep New York City as safe as possible. And then, of course, there are building inspections.

Building inspections are essential to our overall mission, but they don't exactly get you out of bed in the morning. How they work is, each firehouse is responsible for examining all the buildings, both residential and commercial (within certain parameters), within a given area to make sure that they meet the standards established by the fire code; that any combustible materials are stored safely; and that there are no hazards that might hinder or endanger firefighters if they need to operate in the building during a fire. For a firefighter, this is about as unexciting as it gets. You carry a clipboard instead of a Halligan tool. Instead of gratitude, you get attitude. In short, most young firefighters go on building inspection and immediately think, I suffered through the Rock for *this*?

For all its tedium, however, building inspection is vitally important in order to realize the FDNY's objectives. In fact, firefighters fought hard for things like fire codes and building inspections. (Though he'd lobbied the city for years to let him establish a fire code, it wasn't until after the horrific 1911 Triangle Shirtwaist fire that Chief Edward Croker was successful in convincing the city to impose a fire safety code on all New York City buildings.) As a leader, I want my people to be just as high tempo, just as engaged in this aspect of their job as they are when the bells go off and they're called out on a run.

So what I do to make sure people work as hard at building inspection as they do when battling a three-alarm fire is to align the natural drive and enthusiasm they feel whenever they get the chance to work toward their personal goals—which for most of them is to become an experienced and respected firefighter—with the objectives of the organization. And the way I do this is really very simple. At the start of an inspection, as we walk into the building, the first thing I do is pull them aside and ask them how they'd approach this structure if it was already on fire. And just like that, I've got them looking at this situation in terms of their own goals. As we continue through the building, I keep pressing them, using questions to keep making the connection between an actual working fire and the fire code status in this particular building. How would this jammed fire door affect your strategy? What about the fuel oil on the basement floor? So now they're really scrutinizing the building because they suddenly understand how boring, tedious building inspection is directly related to their goal of being a great firefighter.

Outcome #3: Your People Feel That Their Environment Is Positive and Enables Them to Do Their Best Work

I've shown you how transparency, teaching, and open communication make it possible to align people's personal goals—the "What's in it for me?"—with the organization's objectives. As you work toward the first two outcomes, as well as the third—creating a positive environment where people feel they're able to do their best work—you'll find that, together, these outcomes help you create a strong, resilient connection with your people that will give you the authority to lead them to ever higher levels of performance.

I know that there's a temptation to dismiss things like a positive work environment as part of the softer, and so somehow less important, side of leadership. However, look back on your own experiences and think of times when you worked in a place where the air was thick with pessimism, fear, and suspicion. Do you feel that this was a place in which you did your best work? And even if the fear motivated you in the short term, was it sustainable, or did people burn out?

Now, don't get the wrong idea. It's not like we sit in a circle on the apparatus floor banging drums and talking about our childhood. But we do generally make an effort to keep the atmosphere in the firehouse very upbeat. We do it because we think our people work harder if they're happy, or at least not downright miserable. And there have been several studies indicating that when people feel good about the atmosphere at work, they're more productive. Daniel Goleman even argues that positive feelings boost rational thought, enhancing our ability to make complex decisions and be more flexible and creative in our reasoning. Other benefits include better retention, higher morale, and increased motivation and commitment.

So what factors contribute to the climate at work? Well, to put it simply, the factors include . . . you. In fact, 50 to 70 percent of how employees perceive their workplace can be laid at their leaders' feet.

For example, psychologists observing the behavior of groups ranging from gorilla families to small corporate teams have concluded that group members naturally look to their leaders for direction, and not just direction in what to do but in how to feel. You've probably seen this happen countless times in the real world. For instance, nothing deflates optimism and creativity faster than a grim, pessimistic leader. In the FDNY, officers always make a point of appearing upbeat and encouraging around their people, particularly when they're in the thick of a blaze. We know that the moment we show even a touch of doubt or uncertainty, our men will stop thinking about how they're going to beat this fire and start to notice that there are about fifty different ways they could get killed in the next few seconds.

The upshot of all this is that whether you know it or not, you have an incredibly powerful effect on your people. They look to you for cues on how to feel about different situations, objectives, and even people. Rather than ignore or dismiss this power, embrace it and leverage it to its fullest. Of course, this doesn't mean trying to manipulate your people with an insincere or fake attitude. If you try that approach, people will lose confidence in you; manipulation is a definite trust killer. To positively manage your employees' mood and the emotional atmosphere of the group, you need to start (once again) with a foundation of self-awareness and social awareness.

How You Act Affects How Your People Work

Initially, self-awareness is helpful when figuring out what kind of tone you're currently transmitting to your people. In addition to using insight, self-questioning, and empathy to try and imagine how others might perceive your emotional cues, you should, as always, recruit allies who will give you the straight scoop on how you come across to the troops. In the beginning you're concerned not so much with projecting a positive emotional tone as with making sure you're not sending out an oppressively negative vibe. This is because negative emotions such as anger, anxiety, frustration, or a sense of futility or inadequacy disrupt your people's ability to do the more sophisticated kinds of work we do today.

Goleman uses the term *dissonance* to describe the effect of these negative emotions. According to him, because of the way our brains are organized we're still affected by all the old emotional responses that we relied on in our hunter-gatherer days—what are usually called the "flight-or-fight" responses. And even though we don't face off against saber-toothed tigers that much anymore, our brain still resorts to these old responses to deal with any perceived threat, such as layoffs or a boss that seems "out to get me."

The upshot is, anytime any of us feel threatened, we become flooded with survival responses such as anger and hostility that suppress our more noble (and more useful) characteristics. (Remember how threatened I felt by Billy?) Skillful leaders can make use of these survival responses in some situations by harnessing the energy and focus they confer on people. But if the atmosphere of your group is so negative that people are constantly overwhelmed by these survival reactions, then you'll always be facing resentment, disunity, infighting, and hostility. And the only way to keep these toxic fumes from poisoning your leadership efforts is to start using your leadership influence to promote a more positive, productive environment.

How Can I Create a Positive Environment?

In addition to self-awareness, a positive environment also requires social awareness. Instead of just scrutinizing your own attitudes, assumptions, and actions, to be socially aware you need to be clued in to the social dynamics of your own office, for example, its politics, decision networks, and influencers. Social awareness also requires empathy, which enables you to assess your people's emotional state and decide whether or not they're being affected by any negative dynamics in the workplace. Just as with self-awareness, you can't rely solely on your own perceptions. You need to enlist the help of other leaders—both official and unofficial—who won't be afraid to tell you what's really going on.

The key to turning around a nasty emotional atmosphere is to first acknowledge your power. You are, after all, the leader. Everyone looks to you for direction. If you're grumpy and stressed out, chances are they will be too. If you show resignation in the face of daunting challenges or new corporate initiatives, they'll throw in the towel. However, since the opposite is also true, it's time you recognized what an impressive leadership tool emotions can be.

To rehab a battered work environment, it's not enough to use discipline and self-control to dampen your negative tendencies. You've also got to model behaviors that spread feelings of well-being and optimism. So be quick to praise your people. Treat mistakes as teaching opportunities. Express your confidence in your employees. Tell stories about people within your group who've acted in heroic ways while pursuing organizational objectives. These stories will not only lift morale but also set new, inspiring standards of excellence.

There's one more thing you can do to create a positively charged, high-productivity atmosphere. Let people have some fun. Laughter, humor, and joking around are all great ways to release stress and anxiety. Studies show that laughter and play can have an enormous positive impact on people's sense of well-being and ability to do effective work. I call this "the firehouse effect." Firefighters are notorious for their good humor and readiness to laugh or crack a joke. I'm sure there's a connection between the high-stress nature of the work we do and the fact that, on average, most firehouses sound more like a comedy club than a place where men know that every time they go to work they might not come back. Understand, however, that I'm not saying that you need to play Jay Leno for your people. You simply need to give them permission to laugh and have fun at the same time that they're doing great work. And giving permission is simple. Just laugh along once in a while, and your people will handle the rest of it.

A word of caution, however: you don't achieve these outcomes by being your people's buddy. Teaching them and making sure their work environment is conducive to performance does not mean being one of the guys. As a leader, you need to be prepared to be unpopular in order to accomplish your mission. Ask yourself this: do you want to be loved, or respected? If you want to be loved, get a dog.

We've seen how creating strong connections with your people makes it possible to focus them on producing value for your organization's customers. However, in the course of making these connections it's a good bet that you'll sometimes find yourself on unfamiliar ground. When this happens, just remember to keep steering by the same three commitments: following the smoke, treating your people as assets, and developing leaders at all levels.

Following the smoke and uncovering reality leads to self-awareness, social awareness, and self-management. Viewing your people as assets means you'll be more likely to build relationships with them as a means of uncovering their knowledge and expertise. And finally, by developing other leaders throughout your organization you create a corps of supporters who help you manage your group's emotional outlook.

By now you're beginning to see how the approaches I've covered in this book intersect and overlap and build on one another. The next chapter is no different. In it you'll discover how to take what you've learned so far and apply it to making the right decisions, even when the heat is on.

Straight from the Chief

The keys to connecting with your people are, first, establishing a shared point of reference that allows for clear, two-way communication; second, understanding their goals; and third, teaching them about the organization and allowing them to do their best work. After you've got this connection in place, then you're ready to start teaching your people about how their own goals are linked to the organization's goals. And once they understand this connection, you'll be better able to focus all their energy and potential on achieving those goals.

- To figure out what your people's goals are, all you have to do is ask. But before you do, make sure you're ready to listen to what they tell you and understand where they're coming from. To encourage a more candid conversation, ask them open-ended questions; these will spark a dialogue, as opposed to a yes or a no answer.
- Each of your people has a specific job to do, and each job is tied into the larger purpose of the organization. Use each person's job to teach him about the organization and what its goals are. Show him how what he does relates to both the bigger picture and his own aspirations.
- Don't be negative in front of your people. Attitudes are contagious, and if your downbeat mood infects the work environment, it will depress your people's ability to get their work done.

CHAPTER 7

Making the Right Call
When the Heat Is On

How do you make the right decisions?

Fire is an unpredictable enemy. Even when you think you've seen everything it can throw at you, it'll do something that proves you've still got a lot to learn. For example, the radiated heat from a fire can ignite buildings across a street ninety feet wide. Wind-borne embers can stay aloft for miles and miles, sparking new catastrophes in far-off towns and cities and forests. Fire can jump from roof to roof and infiltrate skyscrapers through conduits and air ducts. Even with all our high-tech gear and advanced techniques and strategies, the best defense against such an unpredictable enemy is still the ability to stay one step ahead of it through fast, accurate decision making.

That reminds me of a fire in a Queens supermarket a few years ago. The supermarket manager met the apparatus as it pulled up in front of his store. He explained, almost apologetically, that there was a faint smell of smoke inside the store, hardly worth calling the department about; might even be his imagination. Now, when you're an officer on a call, before you can make any decisions about how to handle a particular incident, you need to follow the smoke. You need to gather information on the location of the fire, the size of the fire, the possible danger to human life, the building construction, your resources in terms of water and personnel, and the type of building, among other things. Clearly, the officer needed more than the store manager's opinion before he could make any meaningful decisions about strategy or tactics.

The officer dispatched a company of firefighters inside the supermarket to search for a possible fire. As Muzak and a faint haze of smoke drifted down from the ceiling, firefighters moved through the aisles, evacuating the shoppers and pushing up the ceiling panels. In checking above the panels the firefighters were examining the cockloft, or space between the ceiling panels and the roof, but none of them found any trace of fire there, just the same light smoke conditions.

Like any good leader, making sure he has access to information from a number of sources and perspectives, the officer then deployed a team of men to the roof. The supermarket was a noncombustible structure; it had steel or concrete walls, floors, and framework. One of the dangers with this type of building, however, is that the roof, which is made of combustible material such as asphalt or paper, is supported by steel trusses or joists as opposed to solid beams; that basically means the possibility of collapse is far greater. As soon as they hit the roof, the firefighters radioed back to report that they had smoke venting from a small pipe, which had to be coming from the same cockloft area the interior men were looking at.

Puzzled, the officer checked back in with his interior team, but the story was the same: no fire in the cockloft, and not much smoke either. From where they were standing, it didn't look too serious. Meanwhile, the rooftop firefighters had cut a small examination hole and found—surprise!—heavy flames lashing at the underbelly of the roof deck, again in what had to be the cockloft. And yet the interior firefighters were still reporting nothing but light smoke.

By taking into account all this information, the officer was able to deduce that the supermarket had a double roof—at some point, rather than replace or repair the original roof, the owners had simply built a new one on top of the old one, thereby creating two separate voids. Having followed the smoke and uncovered the reality of the situation, the officer was able to order the appropriate attack, and the fire was quickly extinguished. But the lesson here is in the way the officer approached the problem: he gathered information from a number of different sources, pulling on his people's unique perspectives, in order to make a final decision that would put them in position to succeed.

Basically, decision making is about taking action now in order to give yourself and your organization a shot at the best possible future. The ability to make decisions is a prerequisite of leadership, but at the same time, decisions themselves can leave you and your organization vulnerable and exposed to failure. By adopting processes and attitudes that support effective decision making, you can minimize the risk and position your organization for long-term growth and success.

DON'T BE AFRAID TO ACCESS YOUR PEOPLE'S EXPERTISE

We love the romantic notion of the leader, off by himself, wrestling with the big decisions. I think this image appeals to our need for leaders to know everything. Unfortunately, not only is this conception of leadership totally unrealistic, it also gets new leaders in a lot of trouble, because for leaders to be successful, they have to recognize that while they don't have all the answers, their people just might. After all, they're the ones down there, day after day, in the trenches. They know how things really work, which strategies are most effective, and which priorities make the most sense. In the FDNY, for example, we make sure our people play a very prominent role in operations; in fact, we make a point of including them in the process as we formulate our strategies and decisions.

In some ways, our focus on mission demands that our officers overcome their egos and draw on the expertise and perspectives of the people around them. For example, during another of the nineteenth century's monstrous fires, Chief Engineer Cornelius Anderson went so far as to assemble his predecessors so he could ask their advice on how to overcome the blaze. While this might have been seen as a sign of weakness in some organizations, Anderson's focus on the department's mission—the need to preserve the city and keep it safe—overwhelmed any considerations of pride or appearance. And it's the same today. When my boss Deputy Chief Mulrenan shows up at a fire that warrants his attention, he doesn't start throwing his weight around and countermanding my orders, although he has the authority to do so. Instead he asks for my observations and my opinion of the situation, just as I gather info from my company officers, and they from their firefighters.

WHAT DOES DISSENT HAVE TO DO
WITH MAKING BETTER DECISIONS?

There are two ways to unlock what your people know. The first is by making them accountable for the success or failure of their piece of the operation. But we'll get to accountability later. For now, let's just look at the second way, which is to use discussion, debate, and questioning to uncover their specific knowledge or viewpoint—or to put it another way, to provoke them through disagreement and dissent, so they'll overcome that bite-your-tongue sort of caution most people have around the boss, and tell you what they really think.

Wait. Did I just say you should *ask for* disagreement? Absolutely. Encourage your people to tell you what they think, even if they think you're wrong. Uncovering your people's unique points of view allows you to examine all possible sides of a problem and test the assumptions on which you might base your decision. I always say that if you're planning strategy with five people, and four of them say, "Yeah, great, Chief," but one says, "What? You're kidding, right?" then that's the guy I want to talk to. I want to know what he sees that I may be missing. Why? Because the more sides you can see of the situation, the more likely it is that you'll hit on the optimal solution.

Dissent does not, however, mean you're trying to stir up ill will among your people, or between yourself and your followers. When I was captain of 48 Engine, I decided that all our probies would work the chart for ninety days. Why? Because "working the chart" would rotate the probies through the tour schedule in such a way that they'd get a chance to work with most of the firefighters in the company. This was important in order to get them time with as many of the company's firefighters as possible and also to give them a sense of how the schedule worked. Now, a few weeks after the policy took effect, one of my senior men came to talk to me about it. Apparently some of the probies were having trouble with the schedule, primarily for reasons related to their personal lives, so he suggested that I cut the period back to sixty days or even thirty.

I listened to what this veteran firefighter had to say. And his rationale made sense. When he was through, I discussed the matter with him, more or less repeating his argument so he'd know I'd heard and understood his perspective. Then I explained to him why I was going to stick with the original policy, why I thought it was important in terms of the job and the probies' development. Finally, I thanked him for coming to me and let him know that I valued his perspective.

Even though this firefighter didn't change my mind, I still wanted him to feel that what he did was worthwhile. You see, by welcoming disagreement, you chip away at some of the complacency that comes with any established organization, whether it's a rescue unit or a large corporation. I don't have to tell you that people sometimes get behind an idea, not because it's good, but because of who thought of it (their boss), who will directly benefit from it (themselves), or who pressured them to go along with it (everyone else). And it's no secret that people spend lots of time hustling to cover up or spin information that they think their bosses might not want to hear. When you're the king, no one wants to tell you something's rotten in the kingdom.

The problem is, when people hoard, suppress, or whitewash information, they diminish the number of future opportunities available to the organization. And the only way to make sure people don't do these things is to encourage honest debate and disagreement. In addition to uncovering valuable information, debates create a kind of cross-pollination of ideas and thoughts, firing up your people's imagination and helping them to make new connections and generate unforeseen alternatives. Naturally, all these things will directly benefit you in your role as key decision maker.

But what about your people? How do they benefit from this approach? Interestingly enough, instead of making them feel ground down by the constant disagreement and (probably) heated debate, a little conflict will actually give your people more confidence and a greater sense of security.

Why? Because conflict has a way of throwing ideas and strategies into the fire to see if they can stand the heat. Debate is a way of testing different ideas and solutions, uncovering their weaknesses and affirming their strengths. When people not only see this firsthand but get to take part in it, they're able to verify for themselves how it works. To return for a moment to some of the concepts we discussed in the chapter on trust, debate is actually a kind of transparency: when people can participate in decision-making discussion and debate, the results gain immense credibility. Your employees will come away committed to executing your decisions because they're allowed to trust in the process that created them. And if certain employees criticize or badmouth a decision, then the rest, who participated in the process, will defend it as if it were their own.

HOW TO TEACH YOUR PEOPLE TO BE DISAGREEABLE (IN A GOOD WAY)

If you want to transform your people from yes-men and -women into partners who aren't afraid to tell you what they really think, you have to set the stage for these new behaviors. Remember, you and your actions serve as points of reference for your people. And while you can emphasize positive behavior (for instance, you can encourage collaboration by making a point of working with others), it's trickier to try and model disagreement; for example, there's a chance your people would think you were shooting down someone's idea not to encourage discussion, but for personal reasons (perhaps because you didn't like the person).

In the department, it's usually enough to simply ask our people for their input. They're all pretty confident, and they . . . well, let me put it this way, you don't have to drag an opinion out of a firefighter. Each has a special background, education, and expertise. Some are college educated, with degrees in the sciences or engineering, while others come from trades such as steelwork or construction. Many have military experience. In the FDNY, you can work with any engine, truck, squad, or rescue company and be confident that there's a wealth of knowledge there waiting to be tapped. I often receive reports or phone calls from my company officers with suggestions about equipment, training, and operations, and it's not unusual to be told that some of this feedback originated with a firefighter in the officer's company.

There are also a few simple tricks you can use to set your people loose. The first is to establish a simple rule, such as refusing to end a meeting until each person has expressed a meaningful disagreement with the featured solution. Another is to create the role of "designated disagree-er," a rotating office with the mandate of basically disagreeing with everything. Because this approach relieves the disagree-er of personal responsibility, it comes in handy if you're leading a tight-knit group whose members don't want to get into it with one another, out of a sense of loyalty.

Also—as we saw in previous chapters—meetings, formal training, and other organizational processes give you plenty of opportunities to teach people to be more involved. Imagine if, while discussing ideas for a new product launch, you went around the table and asked each person to tell you exactly what was wrong with the leading idea. And what if you didn't stop there, but then used questions to challenge and push people to really uncover the hidden weaknesses in the idea? Finally, once you felt that your people had gone the distance on an issue, you might step in and, wearing your teacher's hat, help them see how this kind of questioning and disagreement—when used to clarify and strengthen the assumptions on which decisions will be based—is valuable. While they might find it uncomfortable at first, some of your people would quickly catch on to what you were after, and the new behavior would soon make its way through the group.

After teaching your people how to disagree with you, keep after them to tell you what they really think by asking them open-ended questions and listening to their answers. Be sure to praise those who come back at you with a thoughtful insight or observation. Don't forget, though, that sometimes praise and encouragement are not enough; you may have to actually *ask* your people to take issue with the conventional wisdom. In other words, you'll need to tell them straight out what kind of behavior you'd like to see from them, and then continue to repeat this message until it sticks. You're asking a lot of them here, you really are, so they're going to hang back for a while, but when they finally open up and begin to tentatively offer you their real thoughts and opinions, and you listen and respond thoughtfully instead of steamrolling over them, you'll see their trust in you suddenly go through the roof.

Michael Dell, the founder and CEO of the computer giant, describes his own commitment to reality as a desire to "get to the guts of why things happen." He believes that encouraging his people to ask questions and share ideas through open dialogue is the way to keep his company ahead of the curve. Likewise, Secretary of Defense Donald Rumsfeld's leadership style has been described as "equal parts debating club and wrestling match." Though some find it unorthodox, his approach involves taking an extreme position on a particular issue in order to provoke his people into telling him why he's wrong—but also to think about the ways in which he might be right. Rumsfeld himself describes it as "a process where everyone is learning and everyone is contributing. By the time you end up with a product, it's almost impossible to know who it came from or how it evolved."

HOW TO USE INTUITION, INITIATIVE, AND TIMING TO MAKE THE RIGHT CALL

Just as you need to be open to listening to your employees, you also need to listen to yourself. When we talk about things like intuition, a hunch, or a gut feeling, what we're really referring to is our subconscious mind as it analyzes our previous experiences and tells us how those experiences relate to what's happening right now. If you want, you can picture intuition as a hotline to your accumulated wisdom on a certain subject.

The most dramatic example of intuition I can remember happened about five years ago. Fred Gallagher, who has since retired, was a battalion chief in Battalion 41 at the time. He was with Rescue 2 in Brooklyn, which has always been a very busy company, and on this particular night they were handling a working fire, a pretty good job. The interior attack was stalled, but the men were holding their own. There was no reason to believe that the fire couldn't be beaten. Nonetheless, Gallagher felt something wasn't right. Somehow, in his gut, he knew: dozens of bits of evidence that he must have absorbed and pieced together on a subconscious level told him that this building was going to collapse. So he made the decision to evacuate it. He ordered an urgent retreat—"Urgent, urgent, urgent, everybody back out!" Gallagher got all the firefighters out of the building, and three minutes later, it collapsed.

Intuition is great—as I'm sure all of Gallagher's firefighters would agree—but it's only one of many tools you should turn to when making decisions. In other words, don't let intuition become an excuse for inaction. If something about a decision feels wrong—if your gut says stop—then hold off for as long as you can. Try and uncover the basis for your gut feeling. Follow the smoke. Check out the underlying assumptions. Confer with your people, and consult colleagues and superiors whose opinion you trust. And at the end of the day, if you can't find a reason to deviate from your original plan, then go ahead with it.

SOMETIMES, TIMING REALLY IS EVERYTHING

When you gather information and seek out different perspectives before making a decision, what you're really doing is minimizing risk. As I mentioned earlier, decisions make you vulnerable. Every important decision you make exposes you to all sorts of unexpected variables; therefore, the more you know about the factors that might affect your decisions, the more you can do to manage those factors.

Unfortunately, there's no such thing as *enough* information, and the longer you wait, holding out for that one extra bit of data, the more likely it is that the moment for the decision will already have come and gone. This is why timing is an integral part of decision making. You can do everything else right, but if your decision is poorly timed, the opportunity it might have captured will be long gone.

On September 11, Lieutenant Bob Bohack was the covering officer at 5 Engine, on East Fourteenth Street. He and his company reported to the command post in the lobby of 1 World Trade Center within ten minutes of the first alarm and were ordered to the seventieth floor to prepare for an interior attack. As they climbed the stairs, Bohack heard from evacuating civilians that the second tower had been hit. He also heard rumors—for example, that thirteen more planes were headed for New York City.

After the company reached the nineteenth floor, each man lugging sixty pounds of gear, one of the firefighters of 5 Engine began experiencing chest pains. To make matters worse, another firefighter, a young go-getter, had climbed ahead of them and was now beyond radio contact, which was limited by the building itself. Now Bohack had a decision to make: to keep going, or fall back? After assessing the information he had—"We've got a guy with chest pains, we're getting hit with missiles, there's twenty floors of fire in this building, there's jet fuel burning. This is a losing battle"—he decided to fall back. It wasn't until after they'd emerged from the north tower that Bohack discovered that the south tower had already collapsed. In fact, the lieutenant and his men managed to withdraw only a few blocks before the north tower came down. Only Bohack's initiative and timing saved the lives of his men.

Timing itself is the result of three things: your ability to gather information; your willingness to listen to your intuition; and your initiative. For example, if your decision involves entering some new market, then gathering information on current market trends can help you figure out *when* to act. In the same way, your past experiences, usually expressed through your intuition, add texture and nuance to the decision-making process. And initiative enables you to recognize an opportunity and take risks in order to seize it.

Ultimately, if you want to become a better decision maker, you need to first become a better failure. This is particularly important for leaders. When you fail, or make mistakes, it means (barring basic incompetence) that you're opening yourself up to new experiences and pushing your personal envelope. Mistakes accelerate your personal growth. James Burke, the former CEO of Johnson & Johnson, observed that "it's essential in leading people toward growth to get them to make decisions, and to make mistakes." Of course, mistakes are not only an indication that you're trying to achieve new and better things; they also give you the chance to learn. As they say in the marines, the only unforgivable mistake is the one you've made before.

HOW CAN YOU MAKE SURE YOUR DECISIONS ARE THE BEST THEY CAN BE?

Your goal here is not to learn to make one or two good decisions, but to become a leader who consistently makes the right call. So you need a process that you can rely on to bring you to the optimal decision, again and again, no matter what the circumstances. In this section we're going to explore in detail the phases of this process. It begins with gathering information about the kind of decision you're faced with, then defining what the decision needs to accomplish, and finally, making sure the decision actually gets implemented.

But before we dive in, let's step back and think about the kind of decisions you should be focusing on. Too many leaders, particularly those with micromanaging tendencies, feel compelled to make every possible decision, large and small, that falls within their authority. While this may make them feel valiant and indispensable, the fact is they're not only killing morale by making their people feel useless and inadequate, they're also shortchanging themselves. The really important decisions get neglected while these leaders squander their attention on a thousand minor problems. Effective leaders don't make a truckload of decisions; instead, they focus on the few that make a difference. So here's a simple test: if a decision *can* be made by someone beneath you, then *that person should make it*.

The decision-making process I want to recommend is very flexible; it can be scaled up or down to fit just about any situation. It's as effective for unique problems as it is for generic ones. Also, with only four steps, it's incredibly simple to learn. This makes it the perfect thing for you to teach to your people, not only so they can use it in their own work, but also because it allows you to establish a common decision-making language. Study, remember, and practice this process, and you'll find that any problem, no matter how thorny, can be overcome using this same four-step prescription: *Observe—Orient—Decide—Act*.

Observe

I've already talked quite a bit about the importance of gathering information and following the smoke, so it should come as no surprise that the four-step decision-making process is going to kick off in this same vein. The first step is not only about observation, but also all of the methods by which you can uncover reality and follow the smoke, including engaging your people in discussion, encouraging debate, teaching and questioning, market research, and quantitative analysis.

When I arrive at an incident, I not only look at how the fire is acting, what sort of building is involved, and whether there's any sign of people trapped inside; I also deploy firefighters and officers into the building, to the roof, and to all other exposures so I can benefit from their observations and expertise. At this stage what you want is to create a three-dimensional view of the problem; the more informed and nuanced your grasp of the fundamental issues, the more likely it is that your decision will be the right one.

Orient

To orient yourself is to position yourself in relation to your surroundings. Orienting yourself means evaluating the information you gathered during the observation phase in order to figure out where you are before your decision and where you want to be after your decision (whatever that may be) is carried out. This means you've got to ask yourself: What will it mean to solve this problem? What will have to happen in order for the solution or decision to be successful? The answers to those questions become the standards by which the effectiveness of your decision will be measured. The more precisely you orient yourself—the more exact your standards—the more likely it is that your decision will solve the problem it was meant to solve.

For example, let's say I've got a fire in an MD (multiple-residence dwelling). There are reports of people trapped on the fourth floor, and the fire is in danger of spreading to the building next door. Okay, so I've got a decision to make here. But first I have to orient myself in this particular situation. How will I know when the problem has been resolved? What are the standards of action? Well, based on the information I've gathered and on my knowledge of the FDNY's mission, my decision should be one that results in the rescue of those trapped citizens, the safe extraction of my firefighters, and the containment of the fire itself. There are different ways I could go about meeting those standards of action, different strategies I could implement and tactics I could prescribe, but all of them will have to live up to the same standards in order to be considered *good* decisions. For example, if I put out the fire but the people die, then my decision will have failed to meet its standards of action and, all other things being equal, couldn't be considered a good call on my part.

We all hate to be wrong, but that doesn't give you permission to shy away from putting your standards through the ringer. In fact (for those situations where you have the time), you should write down your standards so that you can really get your hands on them and examine them closely. Accurate standards of action are the basis for a useful decision. If you don't have enough information, or you misinterpret the information you do have, then you'll end up with inappropriate, off-target standards. Which is a wordy way of saying that this is why you have to continue following the smoke throughout the orientation phase as a way of double-checking the integrity of your first-round assumptions.

Decide

In this phase you'll come up with several possible options and then choose the one that has the best chance of satisfying your standards. Again, get your people's input; use disagreement and dissent to shake their good ideas out of them; ask them questions that will stimulate their imagination and inspire innovative solutions. However, once you've decided on a course of action, your people should understand that the time for disagreement is past. After I've consulted with the captain or lieutenant, and I tell an engine company to head to the third floor and knock down that fire, they go. Likewise, once you've made your final decision, commitment is your people's only acceptable response.

I don't want to forget to tell you this, so here: don't forget that you can also decide to do nothing. Sometimes, when the risks of action outweigh the benefits, inaction is a valid decision. Only when inaction will cause a situation to fall apart, or an opportunity to be lost, do you absolutely have to act.

Act

Forget for a moment that you can decide to do nothing. Most decisions are made because someone wants to make something happen.

However, if you make a decision but don't take the steps necessary to make sure it gets implemented, then you haven't really done anything, have you? To be of any use at all, decisions need to have some kind of impact on the situation or problem that they're supposed to address. The process of making sure your decisions matter is called execution. Execution is a catchall that takes in everything you might do in order to make sure a decision gets carried out. Remember, no decision is ever complete until you make someone accountable for its execution, clarify the intermediate objectives that need to be met, and specify when you should be updated on its progress.

WHAT DO YOU HAVE TO DO TO MAKE SURE YOUR DECISIONS GET EXECUTED?

Execution starts with accountability. In other words, if you're going to be an effective decision maker, you need to make sure that someone has accepted the responsibility for getting a particular decision implemented. This might sound pretty obvious, and I wouldn't even mention it if we weren't all guilty of doing just opposite—of making decisions without assigning or accepting accountability. Why do we do it? Maybe we're reluctant to assign responsibility because we're afraid that our people won't rise to the occasion. Or maybe it's because we know deep down that this particular decision is completely impractical or impossible, and that's something we don't want to face.

Whatever the reason, it's time we all got over it. Too many decisions fail because the decision makers don't know how to execute, and that's not a good thing, because ineffectual execution builds cynicism and mistrust among employees and customers alike.

You get to accountability through clear, simple, and thorough communication. You start by designating someone to carry out the decision. Then you explain, as specifically as possible, what objectives he needs to achieve. Define for him exactly what sort of outcome you're expecting, but also set an appropriate number of intermediate objectives you can use to measure his progress. Any ambiguity here can have disastrous consequences, so make sure that your plan of execution answers the following questions:

- Who has to know about the decision?
- What is the desired outcome?
- Who is responsible for achieving this outcome?
- What resources are needed to achieve this outcome, and are those resources available?

One more thing your people should know is when to update you on their progress. Part of execution means continually comparing what's really happening against what you expected to happen. You give yourself the chance to make these comparisons by setting intermediate objectives, or milestones. These milestones are opportunities to check in with your people and see how things are going. Each one of them should mark some meaningful progress toward the final outcome. If you establish trivial or expedient milestones, or too many of them, your people will feel that you don't trust them or have confidence in them; on the other hand, if they cover too much territory or there are too few of them, you may not be able to uncover a problem until it's too late.

I was at a fire recently, a second-alarm that broke out in a two-story commercial building. The companies had encountered the blaze on the second floor and were attacking it, but to knock it down they needed some ventilation; they needed someone to open up the roof for them. Venting a building, by cutting a hole in the roof or knocking out windows or doors, creates a convection effect and draws some of the heat and smoke out of the building, just like a chimney. It also provides an outlet for the pressure building up in the room, making it possible for an engine company to open a hose on the fire without the fire pushing back at them. I dispatched a squad to the roof to take care of it, making sure that the squad officer checked in with me when he had finished cutting the vent.

A few moments later I got a call from the squad officer saying that they'd completed the hole and were beginning to cut a trench. Now, a trench is a specific tactic we use to cut off a fire that's spreading through a building. It's almost like plowing a furrow into the roof, a three-foot-wide, wall-to-wall firebreak. It's basically a longitudinal vent that constrains the fire's spread. However, based on all the information I was receiving, including what I got from the squad officer himself, we didn't need a trench, we just needed to enlarge the original vent. So that's what I told him to do. This is an example of how delegation needs to be used in combination with progress reports that give you the chance to intervene if you need to.

In addition to making sure you get regular updates from your people, you should also venture out from behind your desk and take an in-person look at the results of your decisions. There's no substitute for direct experience. The goal here is to arrive at an honest, warts-and-all appraisal of the execution effort; but if you're too busy to do this on a regular basis, then you should at least send someone that you trust to conduct an in-depth, pull-no-punches survey. In many ways, gathering feedback is a lot like what you did during the observation phase, except that in this case, you're looking for info that will help you evaluate your own decision-making abilities.

Decision making as I've defined it in this chapter is more than simply making choices; it's the process of creating new opportunities. We've seen the different ways in which you can draw on the information and insight of your people. We've examined the roles that intuition, initiative, and timing play in the effectiveness of your decisions. In addition, throughout our study of this process, we've touched on several points where the links between our three commitments and the process of making decisions become more obvious. For example, a commitment to uncovering reality is important if you want to make good decisions. Also, by treating people like assets you'll be more likely to evaluate and hire them in terms of how their qualities will help your organization, as opposed to how much they remind you of yourself or your friends. And you'll find yourself turning to other leaders, both official and unofficial, whenever you need someone to take responsibility for executing an important decision.

In fact, execution is the most important—and for some bizarre reason, most overlooked—aspect of leadership. That's why in the next chapter we're going to focus specifically on what you can do to master the art of effective execution.

Straight from the Chief

Making decisions that require you to do more than just slap a routine solution on a problem is what leadership is all about. The ideal decision-making process is one that asks you to figure out what the real problem is (that is, to uncover the reality, or follow the smoke), orient yourself in relation to the problem, make a choice, and then execute it.

- Your people are often your best source of information, and conflict is the most efficient way of shaking their perspectives and insights out of them. Use questions and devil's advocate suggestions to encourage discussion and dissent. Ask your people to give you their best disagreement.

- Don't dismiss the roles that intangibles such as intuition, initiative, and timing play in your decision-making process. After all, intuition is really your subconscious trying to offer up the benefits of a lifetime's worth of experience, while initiative and timing are related qualities that, at their core, are about knowing when the benefits of action outweigh inaction.

- There are four steps you should follow when making decisions: Observe—Orient—Decide—Act. The two most important phases of this process are the first (Observe) and the last (Act). If you don't uncover enough or the right kind of information, the whole process is undermined. And if you don't execute, what's the point?

CHAPTER 8

No One Goes Home Until the Fire's Out

How do you lead for execution?

Execution is key because it's the part of leadership that relates not just to getting things done, but to getting the *right* things done. If you can't execute, you can't be effective.

Problems with execution are also signs of a weakness in your leadership approach. This is true in business, and it's certainly true in the fire service. For us, the act of extinguishing a fire—advancing an attack line into a burning building—is our leadership crucible. For us, it's not just success and failure that depend on flawless execution, but life and death.

When you punch a clock with an engine company, you work in hell. Burning embers rain down on you. Waves of smoke as hot as 1,400 degrees Fahrenheit force you to crawl on your hands and knees across carpets of hot ash. (To give you some idea of what 1,400 degrees really means: when your skin is exposed to temperatures of 212 degrees for more than fifteen seconds, you get second-degree burns.) The flames themselves, when you encounter them, are somewhere between 500 and 1,000 degrees, though even an ordinary house fire can push those averages up to around 1,800. Behind you you'll drag hundreds of pounds of fully charged hose, and the instant you open up the nozzle, it's like a rocket, 180 gallons of water per minute blasting you backward. Under such back pressure, the hose twists in your hands and struggles to writhe free.

The water vaporizes the instant it hits the hot flame and smoke. The molecular bonds between the hydrogen and oxygen are shattered, and while this does subtract heat from the fire, the resulting gases immediately expand into a superheated, 500-degree cloud capable of scalding a firefighter even through his protective turnout gear.

Given all the different ways people can get hurt in such a hostile environment, it shouldn't be hard to understand why an interior hose attack requires almost perfect execution. So how do we make sure that caliber of execution happens? Well, we start by making sure we know where the fire is and what the conditions are before we send in our people. We clearly communicate to them what our goals are. We make sure they know whether we want them to attack the fire, or contain it, or simply observe the conditions and report back.

We make sure we have the right people on the line—our bravest, best, and most experienced. If there's a probie in the company, we keep him with us.

We make sure the right resources are available. Is the water pressure sufficient? Are we pulling the right diameter hose for the fire? Is there a supporting company waiting to take up the line if necessary? Do we have a truck company venting the roof, the windows? Do we need to call a second or third alarm?

And we never forget that each situation is unique. So we're constantly revisiting our strategy and tactical plan, and asking ourselves: Are they appropriate? Have we considered what might go wrong, and do we have a response planned? Finally, have we overlooked anything? Is there any information we might have marginalized or dismissed because it didn't fit the expected pattern? Is there any one piece of information we don't have in our hands that would dramatically lower our risk?

FIVE KEYS YOU CAN USE TO UNLOCK EXECUTION

As you can see, execution isn't a single skill or quality. The term wraps its long arms around a range of leadership approaches, many of which we've already discussed. What execution really is is a measure of how well you can deploy those various approaches.

The things we've covered so far—creating trusting environments, forging connections with your people, and teaching them about organizational objectives—are the things that will enable your people to execute effectively. So if things aren't getting done—if your people aren't executing effectively—then, all other things being equal, the problem lies with the leadership you're giving them. In this chapter, I'll focus on the five questions you need to be able to answer yes to, every day, in order to jump-start your people's capacity for effective execution.

Question #1: Are Your Goals Clear?

Communicating clear objectives and outcomes to your people is a prerequisite for execution. In some ways, this goes back to my earlier sections on communication and connection. Too many organizations don't establish a common language for their people, and in the absence of widely understood specific phrases and terms, people fall back on generalizations and subjective language. Directives like "You know what I want," "Do what you did last time," and "Make it happen" are things that should never come out of your mouth.

Instead, shoot for specificity. Describe the outcome you want, using a mix of qualitative and quantitative parameters. The outcome should look like *X*, cost *Y* amount of money, and produce an effect of *Z*. It's the difference between telling people to put out a fire and telling them to vent the room and then stretch four lengths of two-and-a-half-inch hose to the second floor and begin an interior attack. Which one do you think will result in real execution?

You also need to communicate priorities to your people. Priorities are those things that have got to be addressed as part of your execution in order for the whole thing to be successful. For example, in the FDNY our priorities are life, containment, and property, in that order. So even if our goal in executing a decision is to extinguish a fire, we can't do it in such a way that would endanger someone's life.

Deputy Chief Vincent Dunn tells the story of how he once had to change strategies—from an aggressive interior attack to an exterior, defensive containment—and at the same time tells us something about how priorities work. Faced with a fire in a multiple-dwelling building that had blown out a second-story window and was leaping up the building's face, threatening adjoining structures, he decided to withdraw his firefighters, raise an aerial platform, and bombard the fire with a master stream. A master stream is the heavy artillery of the FDNY. Each large-caliber nozzle delivers five hundred gallons of water per minute, which is more than two tons of water every thirty seconds. Improperly used, a master stream can dislodge ceilings, topple chimneys and parapets, and lift the roof off a building. Because of these dangers, and because the use of a master stream definitely increases the risk of collapse (after all, you're adding weight to the building in the form of water, at a rate of 4,150 pounds each minute), all firefighters inside the structure need to be withdrawn before a master stream can be opened.

Dunn watched during the few moments needed to back out the companies as the fire spread to the roof. He could hear the crowd that had gathered muttering about why it was taking him so long to put out the fire. But Dunn was simply observing the department priorities, getting the men out before cutting loose with the big guns. In order to execute effectively in this situation, Dunn had to know the organization's priorities: in this case, lives superseded property.

Question #2: Who's Going to Get It Done?

It's not simply a matter of grabbing a warm body, or a team of warm bodies, and throwing them at a problem. At the very least, you want to have people whose strengths and experience are relevant to the project at hand. By identifying these people early on in the decision-making process and including them in the Observe, Orient, and Decide phases, you create accountability, which strengthens execution.

I think by now most leaders understand that they can't actually *motivate* their people. There's nothing you can do to or for them that will make them want to do something they really don't care about. People can only motivate themselves, and this comes from having a personal stake in something.

However, as a leader, you can give your people this personal stake by including them in the dialogue and planning that makes up the decision-making process. By listening to what they have to say, giving them a voice in refining goals, and including them when coming up with alternatives or contingency plans, you allow them to care about what's going on. It's not pandering to your people when you do these things, or abdicating your own authority; instead, you're allowing them to become personally invested in the outcome of the decision-making process. In other words, you're creating the conditions necessary for them to become accountable for execution.

The best way to see how this approach works is to look at what happens when you don't use it. Go ahead. Exclude people from the decision-making process. Bring them in at the last stage—the Act stage—and give them their marching orders. When you do, what you're basically telling them is that they're nothing more than hired muscle, good only for carrying out orders. This makes them feel that you don't truly value them, and it also makes them frustrated as hell because you're not giving them a chance to use their full range of skills and abilities. When your employees feel unvalued and frustrated, their commitment, performance, and effectiveness all suffer dramatically. But when you allow people to feel that they have some influence over the direction of the organization, when they can feel that they have some say in events that affect them, then you've got them on the way to caring about what happens. And this is where execution begins.

Up until now I've made a case for engaging your people through discussion and debate because it's a good way to tap into their expertise and experience. You can see how this approach creates a collaborative atmosphere and leads to the kind of deep commitment I described earlier. The only problem is, you can't include everyone who might be affected by a decision in the top-level decision-making process. You know that when I'm making a decision at the fire ground, I don't round up every firefighter in earshot. But I do confer with the leaders at the level below mine, and also teach them to do the same for their people. This way, my plan of action goes through continual fine-tuning, becoming more operational as it works down through the ranks.

From my spot at the top of the pyramid, I focus on defining the main objectives, objectives that then flow from leader to leader, each of whom goes through his or her own decision-making cycle, with everything getting more and more operational as it gets closer to the front line. But at each point along the way, the same discussion and debate is guiding the refinement of objectives into specific actions.

I'd like to make one final point on the question of "Who's going to get it done?" It's certainly true that the FDNY, and most other organizations today, use teams to tackle the sort of complex work that's beyond the ability of a single person to accomplish. While you should match the strengths of these teams to the needs of your objectives, you should also try and make sure that the teams are balanced in terms of ability, attitude, and leadership. For instance, we always try to have a senior firefighter on every engine or truck company who can assist the lieutenant or captain and also serve as a focal point for the team in times of stress.

I've read of how some leaders make a point of rotating men in and out of teams to break up cliques and make sure people are comfortable working with a variety of different people. I've also encountered the theory that says when you have a successful team, don't break it up, and do everything possible to strengthen those internal bonds. But based on my experience as an officer in the fire service, I would recommend the former approach. Firefighters will work with different people—within the same firehouse, of course—all the time. This forces them to harmonize their personal styles with different leaders and colleagues, and it also enables the spread of knowledge and skills throughout the firehouse as the firefighters teach and learn from one another. Finally, in the FDNY it's essential that all the firefighters know with absolute certainty that they can rely on their brothers and sisters, and the only way to accomplish that is to make sure each person has firsthand experience working with all the other firefighters in the house.

Question #3: What Are They Going to Use to Get It Done?

Of course, now that you know what needs to get done and who's going to do it, you have to make sure your people have what they need to do the job right. They need resources—including manpower, information, training, and equipment—in order to be effective. You also need to be aware of the areas of your organization that contribute the most to its success, and to channel resources to them as necessary, even if it means starving other sectors.

As a leader, it's your job to make sure your people have what they need to achieve the objectives you've set out for them. I couldn't expect my men to continue to deliver such exceptional performance if I didn't make sure they were properly equipped, trained, and supported each time they answered a call. Obviously, if their resources drop below a certain level—no turnout gear, for instance, or hoses—they won't be able to get much done, and they'll probably hurt themselves while trying to do it. For most of you, a shortfall in resources probably won't have such a grim impact, but it could be bad enough in its own way: continued negligence in a key area will certainly hurt your organization, and during a critical time could cause it to fail completely.

In the FDNY, resource management on the fire ground is the sole responsibility of the incident commander. Initially, the incident commander is the first company officer to arrive on the scene. So if an engine company roars up, as soon as that lieutenant or captain hits the pavement, he's the man. He's the one with the authority to request more resources if he feels that the fire is going to be a two-alarm fire or higher, a working fire.

Now, as soon as the chief officer is on the scene, he becomes the incident commander. At this point, one of his most important jobs is to manage resources. This is because it's very difficult to play catch-up with a fire. The stuff moves unbelievably fast and with an almost malicious ability to surprise you. So the chief officer has got to have the resources on hand to deal with a situation that might evolve in unforeseen ways. If he has to send for more men, more equipment, it could take some time for them to arrive and deploy, since they're coming from areas beyond (sometimes far beyond) the initial alarm territory. Meanwhile, fire can gut a room in fewer then sixty seconds.

So incident commanders constantly monitor the progress of the operation, and based on what they discover, have supporting companies and extra equipment standing by. As one of the instructors for the FDNY Chief Command course, I can tell you that we stress the importance of maintaining adequate reserves. We never want to have just the companies involved with fighting the fire. Instead, we have reserve companies standing by, in full gear, ready to roll in case the fire extends to another area, or we get reports of people trapped by the flames, or a firefighter is reported down or missing. And when those reserves start to be activated, we call in still more reserves.

No leader should conduct operations without being able to quickly access more resources, whether extra staff to fill a rush of orders or new equipment to stay competitive in the industry.

Businesses' continued reliance on cost cutting as a tool to enhance the bottom line probably means that you'll never be able to give your employees all the resources you might like to. Certainly, we're under similar constraints in the fire department. Though I'm constantly fearful of budget cuts or holding out for some extra training or an essential piece of equipment, I also know that the cuts will inevitably come. However, I can make sure they don't undermine our effectiveness any more than necessary by putting my resources where they'll do the most good. For me, this means socking the money into training and equipment. Put your resources where you'll get the most out of them by matching them to opportunities and allotting them to those areas that play the biggest role in delivering results for the organization. Sometimes this will mean making hard choices, such as letting go of opportunities, people, or even whole divisions. It's precisely because these choices are so difficult and have the potential to affect so many people that you need to base your actions on the best information possible; follow the smoke to find out where you're getting the most bang for your buck and you'll be able to maintain your ability to execute while not cutting any more than you absolutely have to.

Question #4: How Is It Going to Get Done?

This question gets to the heart of execution. If you don't have a clear idea of how you're going to get to your objectives—or at least a firm sense of the intermediate goals that point the way to the outcome you want—then you'll probably never get there. So put your objectives to work. Use them to guide you in formulating strategy, and then work with your people to make that strategy operational. Ultimately, you want a strategy specific enough to support a workable operating or tactical plan, but still one general enough to allow you some flexibility in the face of the unexpected.

Strategy, in the classic sense, is a broad, overarching theory of how you're going to achieve your objectives—how you're going to get something done. But it's such a neat, important-sounding word that I can't really blame people for using it to describe so many things other than, well, strategy. I think the most blatant offense here is when people use *strategy* to describe what's really just tactics, or what you could also call an operating plan. But strategy, whether it refers to a new product launch or a rescue operation, simply identifies an objective and the general approach you'll use to reach that objective, while also paying special attention to any aspects of your plan that are unique or essential. For example, if the success of your strategy hinges on using some new technology, such as the Internet, then that's part of your strategy. Likewise, if I decide that we're going to attack a fire using a master stream suppression, then that's part of my strategy. Tactics, or the operating plan, is the *how* of your strategy. It works within your strategy's broad outline to explain how, exactly, you're going to get from *here* to *there*.

While you're the one responsible for deciding on a strategy and making sure your people know what it is, you should resist the temptation to hand them an operating plan at the same time. Although you probably know exactly what you would do to get the results you want, forcing your people to do things your way won't help them develop, or make them feel useful or valued. Your job is to define the objectives they should achieve and the guidelines they should adhere to; after that it's up to your people to decide how they're going to accomplish those things. By giving them the freedom to do things their way, you show them that you trust them and have confidence in them. You also make it possible for them to take ownership of the solution, which gets them involved in things and leads to exceptional execution.

In Afghanistan, for example, when the United States and its allies were moving against the Taliban, Special Forces soldiers were empowered to call in air strikes based only on the mission parameters they'd been given. No one was looking over their shoulder. They didn't need anyone to sign off on their recommendation. They just did it. It's the same in the FDNY. We establish the mission guidelines and priorities, and then we let our people do their jobs. I would never tell a truckie, for example, how to get to the roof, or what equipment to take, or even what to do once he got there. Instead, I'll just tell him I need ventilation on the roof. And I know the job will get done. Does it matter that he might have a different way of going about it than I would? Of course not.

But while you should let your people create the operating plan, you still need to be able to manage it. In this case, your best management tools are milestones. As one definition puts it, operating plans "break long-term goals down into short-term targets." Employed correctly, these short-term targets act like landmarks that can be used to help your people navigate through your strategic plan. They're the tangible pieces of your strategy that help guide your people's efforts.

To be truly useful, however, milestones need to be coupled with some kind of feedback schedule. Reach an agreement with your people on when you'll meet to discuss their progress. In addition to being a great opportunity to teach and gather information from your people, these regular meetings will allow you to uncover any unforeseen obstacles or developing trends that might mean you need to rethink your strategy. On the fire ground, progress reports help the incident commander evaluate his strategy and decisions, and give him opportunities to stop what's going on and change directions.

Give your people a chance to help define the milestones and feedback protocols. (Obviously, this doesn't apply to high-pressure situations—in those instances, you make the calls and your people obey.) By including them in the process, you generate accountability and also get the chance to test the basic assumptions of your strategy. If your people are inexperienced, or are still in the first year of a new position, you may also want to push them to explain to you how they're going to transform your strategy into a working plan. Ask them, for instance, how they're going to accomplish their milestones. If you can see from their response that they're on the road to ruin, help them find the flaws in their plan. Don't just give them the "right" answer; lead them to uncover the problem and then let them formulate their own solution. On the other hand, if you're working with more experienced people, it should be enough to simply establish milestones and a progress report schedule and double-check that they have an operating plan they're confident in.

But regardless of whether your people are seasoned hands or fresh recruits, you should always work with them to create contingency plans. The only thing you can ever be sure of is that nothing is ever for sure. During the Cold War, the fire department's Office of Civil Defense created a number of contingency plans that the department could resort to in case of a nuclear attack. War-game exercises were conducted in order to prepare firefighters for various nightmarish scenarios. Today, of course, in addition to dirty bombs and nuclear weapons, we plan for biowarfare, chemical weapons, car bombs, and other forms of terrorism.

In addition, and on a less spectacular level, officers are always developing contingency plans on the fly, throughout an operation. Certainly I'm always trying to keep a step ahead of events, looking at what needs to get done, what's being done, what we'll have to do if the current approach fails.

When it's a large operation, two or three alarms or more, a deputy chief takes over as incident commander (deputy chief is the rank just above mine). A good friend of mine, Deputy Chief Jim Murtagh, now retired, would often give me advice and take the time to explain lessons he'd learned as a leader. One lesson in particular was about what he as a deputy chief was looking for when he arrived at a serious fire. He told me that he didn't immediately focus so much on what the battalion chief was doing at that moment, but rather, he quickly assessed what tactics might be required and what resources needed if the battalion chief's strategy didn't work. In other words, he was devising contingency plans in case what the battalion chief had going on didn't work out.

You can't plan for every eventuality. So before you embark on some plan of attack, you need to huddle up with your people, uncover the areas that are most vulnerable to some kind of disruption, and then sketch out a compensating course of action. How detailed you want your contingency plans to be is up to you and your people. I know some leaders who are comfortable with just the slightest outline, while others want to have several full-blooded plans fleshed out and agreed on before going forward. It's your call.

Only after you have met with the people accountable for executing your decision, have clarified your objectives, have established your strategy, have agreed on milestones, have set a progress report schedule, and have discussed contingency plans do you get to the most important part of the discussion: the end. In the FDNY, we confirm the details of an operational decision by repeating them back to the person who made that particular decision. For example, if I call Ladder 58 and tell them I've been advised that we have a person in distress in apartment 5C, and say, "Go and get them out," Ladder 58's commander will respond with, "Ladder 58 to Battalion 18, 10-4, Chief, person in distress in apartment 5C." This simple exchange assures both of us that we're on the same page and that execution is under way.

Similarly, in their aptly titled book *Execution*, Larry Bossidy and Ram Charan make a point of recommending, "Never finish a meeting without clarifying what the follow-through will be." By confirming that everyone is in agreement on the plan of attack, you make sure that you're all on the same page. In fact, this is so important that I also recommend you follow up with your people in writing. It doesn't need to be particularly formal; simply let them know how you see the objectives, strategy, milestones, and feedback, plus any operational details or contingency plans you discussed during the meeting. This is your best (and last) opportunity to uncover any inconsistencies or misunderstandings that may bite you later.

Question #5: Does All This Seem Reasonable?

At one time we taught firefighters never to open up the hose on smoke. This was because years ago all the buildings in New York City had single-pane windows. When a fire reached a certain point, the windows would burst from the mounting pressure of the heat inside the room and naturally start venting that heat outside. This meant that not only was the smoke you encountered cooler—you weren't in danger of being burned by it—but it had dissipated enough so that if you crouched down you could see doorways, room layouts, and victims who had collapsed. Since smoke is an aerosol composed of fine particles of soot and suspended droplets of liquid, hitting it with the stream would just stir it all up and turn it into a kind of soup. You'd completely lose your visibility, all the way down to the floor.

However, the thermal pane windows in newer, more energy-efficient buildings don't shatter under temperature stress. These rooms seal in all that heat, and since it has to go somewhere, it's radiated back into the smoke. The result is what's aptly known as hot smoke, smoke that can reach temperatures of fourteen hundred degrees. That's easily hot enough to cause third-degree burns, which can char your skin all the way down to the bone. As a result, we've begun to sometimes open up the stream on smoke, since the water carries the heat away as steam and brings things down to a level where we can operate safely. This is an example of how new information or developments caused us to change our tactics, though without straying from the broader parameters of the mission.

"Does all this seem reasonable?" This is a question that needs to be asked throughout the execution process—not just during the planning stage, but also when your feedback alerts you to new obstacles or unexpected developments. This question should inspire you to go back and review all the ingredients that you need for a successful execution—objectives, people, resources, strategy, and tactics—and make sure that, given what you know or have just discovered, these will still get the job done. Nothing is more ineffective, or frustrating for your people, than wasting time and resources trying to accomplish something that can't possibly be achieved, because your approach is inappropriate or your people aren't prepared or your resources are insufficient. Take it from me: an easy way to improve your effectiveness is just to ask yourself whether the assumptions you've made in these key areas make sense. Your answer will tell you all you need to know about your chances of success.

But you need to do more than start asking yourself these questions *after* the ball is already rolling; wrongheaded or insanely ambitious objectives are probably the biggest reason why organizations have so much trouble with execution. While objectives are absolutely necessary in order to get things done, objectives that aim impossibly high or that simply can't be achieved with your current people and resources are worse than useless. Your people will feel that they're being set up for failure, and you'll end up sapping their enthusiasm, self-confidence, and drive to achieve.

Remember, change is the one thing that never changes. Assumptions that seemed perfectly reasonable when you were coming up with milestones, checking resources, and selecting people can appear hopelessly delusional after some unexpected change in the environment. You need to use the feedback meetings you've built into the execution process as opportunities to constantly test and question the assumptions on which you've based your objectives. New information, sudden obstacles, or unanticipated trends are fresh chances to reexamine plans, milestones, and objectives. Stay flexible. Keep your long-range view focused on the fundamental priorities—those things that create value for the customer—and let the short term become a series of possible routes, contingencies, and detours. Any one of them might become your best chance to accomplish your goals.

Finally, if your feedback process uncovers information that might require a more fundamental rethinking of strategy, don't be afraid to take it to your superior. Even if she doesn't support your execution process with milestones or regular meetings, you now know how important these things are to your ability to get things done effectively. So take the initiative. As a leader, you're responsible for making sure your organization achieves its goals. Whenever you come across information that you feel will require changes in your organization's overall strategy, then part of execution means getting this information to those who can reshape the company's strategic response.

CREATING A CULTURE OF EXECUTION

As you work through these five questions, also pay attention to how your organization's processes and procedures make it either easier or more difficult for your people to get things done. What do I mean by processes and procedures? Well, these are those routines—examples of which include planning, budgeting, employee reviews, and hiring—that your organization uses to keep track of its various operations and make sure that its basic needs are met. In theory, these processes should benefit you, the organization, and your employees equally, but somehow that never quite ends up happening. In many organizations, the processes get so bloated that they obscure their original purpose. The problem, I think, is that without clear links to the organization's mission, objectives, or customers, the meaning behind these processes gets lost.

Not only can you make these processes meaningful again, but you can use them to help you create an execution-oriented culture. Because they're so deeply embedded in the organization, you can hitch a ride on these processes and use them to connect with your people, teach them about the organization and its objectives, and uncover their knowledge and expertise through discussion.

For example, when Jack Welch took over General Electric, he created something he called the CEC, or Corporate Executive Council. This group, composed of the company's best leaders, would meet once a year to grapple with the challenges facing the organization's various businesses and offer Welch counsel. The CEC actually replaced a dysfunctional meeting process in which various heads of business would make sanitized, CYA (cover-your-ass) presentations, to be followed up with a ritual interrogation by the CEO and CFO. Under Welch, the practice was abolished and the CEC took its place in order to provide a forum for exchanging insights and spreading best practices.

Another example of an organizational process that also serves as a teaching vehicle is the Special Forces' after-action review. This process is really just a formalized way of asking the question "What just happened?" Immediately after any exercise or operation, everyone involved, from privates to generals, sits down together to review what transpired and learn from it. We have a similar process in the FDNY, called a postoperational critique. After every operation, we gather at the firehouse and discuss what just went down. Why did so-and-so make that particular decision? What information led him to that conclusion? What was the result? What can we learn from this?

Complementing our postoperational critique is a program called Pass It On, which helps us spread any information uncovered during these critiques to other battalions and companies. Whenever a serious situation or a close call occurs, the details of the incident's critique—such as the possible causes, the actions taken by the officers and firefighters involved, and any recommendations for future action in similar situations—are forwarded to headquarters for review. If everything checks out, then the information is packaged, including photographs, graphics, or maps, and distributed to every firehouse throughout the city so that officers and firefighters can benefit from the lessons learned.

So stop mindlessly supporting your organization's rain dance rituals and turn them into leadership opportunities. Tell people what your new goals are for these moribund meetings and make sure your actions support your words. Break down the adversarial attitudes that hijack the sharing of information between your people. Recognize and praise those who embody a more collaborative approach. As the previous examples demonstrate, these organizational processes don't have to be lifeless exercises; instead, under your guidance, they can become powerful drivers of an execution culture.

Adopting the approaches I've outlined in this chapter will help you get the right things done; deploying them in accordance with the four-step decision-making process we talked about in chapter 7 will dramatically elevate your overall effectiveness. But some questions still remain, such as How can you get people to take responsibility for their actions? How can you actually lead for execution? We'll get to those questions in the next chapter, when we look at the ways in which you can inspire your people to get their hands dirty and make things happen.

Straight from the Chief

It's during the action phase of the decision-making process—also known as execution—that things really get done. It's also where weaknesses in leadership become most apparent. These five questions will help you focus on the key elements of execution:

1. **Are your goals clear?** Make sure you can define your objectives in specific, quantitative terms—these are the standards you'll use to gauge success or failure. Equally important, make sure your people understand what those terms mean. It's not going too far to ask them to explain those standards back to you so you can confirm that they get it.

2. **Who's going to get it done?** You need to put the right people on the right jobs. Match their strengths to the needs of the undertaking.

3. **What are they going to use to get it done?** What resources are needed to accomplish your objectives? Do you have those resources? If not, you'll need to revise your goals.

4. **How is it going to get done?** This question focuses you on your strategy and tactics. Even though you'll almost certainly deviate from this plan, you need to have one if you're to have any chance of succeeding.

5. **Does all this seem reasonable?** First, is what you're asking possible, or are you setting your people up for failure? Second, this question should prompt you to set up a feedback schedule so you can continue to gather information and test your original assumptions in light of what's happening *now*.

CHAPTER 9

Fire Up Your People's Performance

How do you get your people to be
fully engaged in their work?

As a battalion commander, I'm responsible for the 150 men of Engine Companies 45, 48, and 88, and Ladder Companies 38, 56, and 58. While I have a terrific team of very capable leaders—captains, lieutenants, and senior firefighters—who do a lot of the heavy lifting, ultimately I'm accountable for what happens in the firehouses and on the fire ground. If something goes wrong, it's on me.

Because there's so much to keep track of at the chief officer level, all chief officers have an aide. Aides in the fire service are like aides-de-camp or attachés in the military. Typically senior firefighters, aides are responsible for completing paperwork such as reports and notifications; they drive the battalion vehicle to alarms that the chief is assigned to; they adjust and balance the firefighter manpower for the units in the battalion; and they assist with radio communication and progress reports while at the fire ground so the chief can focus on managing the operation. But perhaps most important, the aide expands the chief's range of command. He can cover other aspects of the operation and let the chief know if there are problems developing that need his attention. After seeing all that they do, you can understand why I say that battalion aides play an important leadership role of their own within the organization.

However, I arrived for a night tour not too long ago and discovered that one of the battalion aides had gone home on a previous tour without waiting to be relieved by his replacement. Of course, soon after he left but before his replacement came on duty, an alarm came in, leaving the battalion shorthanded. The commander at that time, who had been affected by this guy's negligence, was upset with the situation, but hadn't taken any action yet. After asking a few questions of other people close to the incident, I called the chief to discuss what we should do. I felt that this was a serious violation that required us to take some action.

To put it more simply, steam was coming out of my ears. We're in the business of saving lives, and there isn't a single job in the fire service that doesn't ultimately, in some way, support that mission. And here this jerk takes it upon himself to upset that balance because he can't be bothered to wait fifteen minutes until his replacement shows up. While the commander was pretty angry as well, he hadn't yet decided how he wanted to handle the situation. For myself, I saw this as a situation that demanded a highly visible response so that the other firefighters could see how their leaders felt about this kind of thing. It's important to remember that everything you do not only affects how your people see you, but also affects how they see themselves in relation to their job. You can make them proud to be working where they are, or you can make them ashamed.

That battalion aide did not last another hour in the battalion. A new aide was brought in the next day. This is not to say that being a leader means getting rid of people. But we've all had jobs where someone wasn't pulling his weight, and in time became a drag on the group's morale and effectiveness. That was the case here, and over the next several days, as the story filtered down through the battalion, many firefighters found ways of letting us know that they appreciated our reasoning.

Now, this may seem like an odd leadership story, but take a closer look and you'll find that it's an example of the kind of quiet, day-to-day leadership that will help you create an execution-oriented culture. In most organizations, the opportunities for high-visibility heroics are few and far between, but the need to demonstrate your rock-steady leadership qualities is a daily job requirement. In this case, I acted out of my profound belief in the importance of the job we undertake as firefighters; the men understood and appreciated this action because it validated and enhanced the stature of their own jobs and allowed them to take pride in doing those jobs well.

In the last chapter we talked about how to prepare for execution by focusing on four key areas: objectives, people, resources, and planning. Now we're going to talk about how to lead for execution. In order to give us some way to talk about leadership, I describe it in this chapter as a ladder, with each rung of the ladder a different leadership principle. As we look at each of the six different rungs and how they lead you toward execution, we'll also see how the approaches we've covered so far—even the three commitments—support the powerful leadership tradition of the FDNY.

The link between preparing for execution and leading for execution is embodied in your organization's objectives. I know I've covered this in earlier chapters; remember that golden oldie "The key to managing for results is making your organization's goals tangible"? By making the connection between company objectives and personal goals explicit and comprehensible to each of your people, you can turn employees into partners, align everyone's efforts, and answer their all-important, burning question: "What's in it for me?"

Describing organizational objectives in a way that seems relevant to people's personal goals is what's referred to as having a leadership vision. Based on conversations I've had over the years, I feel that business leaders in particular have had problems with "the vision thing." The main cause, I think, is that most examples of vision have come from military or political history, where the leader's vision was rooted in loftier notions than customer value or productivity. I can't imagine Patton rallying the troops with the prospect of making the second-quarter numbers. But vision doesn't have to be grand or historic. Vision is nothing more than describing your organization's goals in a way that will mean something to your people and inspire them to action. So it stands to reason that a meaningful vision is one that emphasizes your people's goals and motives.

Some people act as if just having a vision will motivate others. If your vision is sufficiently compelling, or so the story goes, your people will be falling over themselves to help you achieve your goals. But when managers and bosses talk about motivation, they're really referring to the age-old problem of trying to get their people to do the things they want them to do. We beat our heads against the wall trying to think of ways to motivate our people; we hire consultants and read books and pray.

But the truth is, you really can't just *get* a person to do something he doesn't want to do. I mean, you can try: there are a number of popular methods available, though they're really just some kind of coercion or manipulation. Fear, for example, works for a bit, but makes enemies of your people in the long run. You can also try setting very high standards and pushing your people relentlessly to achieve them, but this usually ends in burnout. Even money isn't a particularly effective motivator. Studies have shown that while underpaying people definitely reduces motivation, paying them more money doesn't increase motivation, productivity, or effectiveness.

The only real way to motivate your people is to offer them the chance to succeed. For most firefighters, being successful means being successful at their job, at saving lives. So in the FDNY, we motivate people by giving them the chance to go to the "good" fires (it might sound crazy, but to a firefighter, a good fire is the risky, life-threatening blaze most people want nothing to do with), to be involved in emergency operations, to prove themselves in front of their peers, and to earn the group's respect. But even if your people aren't firefighters, their idea of success is still defined by the goals they've achieved or dreams they've realized. The best way to fire them up is to give them the chance to work toward their goals.

THE FIRST RUNG: SET EXPECTATIONS

I've been hammering away at the importance of connecting with your people and teaching them about your organization's mission and objectives, and though these things are essential to execution, that's not what I'm talking about here. What I want to focus on now is how you can use *expectations* to challenge and motivate your people.

The first thing you need to do with expectations is make sure they're clear. There can't be any fuzziness about them, which is why measurements are so handy when establishing expectations. It's one thing to say to an employee, "I expect you to focus on customer satisfaction," and quite another to say, "I expect you to raise your level of customer satisfaction by five percent." Be explicit about what you expect of your people, particularly when it comes to the measurements you'll be using to gauge their success.

I think most managers and leaders get this, but what some don't seem to understand is that expectations can't be standardized; it's ridiculous to insist on a standard for a group of individuals who all have their own unique strengths and talents. Try to apply expectations to all employees equally and what you get is an average. And since there's no incentive for your best people to exceed these average expectations, they don't; they work up to the prescribed level of mediocrity and then stop. In other words, broad, undifferentiated standards end up *lowering* the quality of your people's work.

To wipe out this creeping blandness, you need to work with your people one-on-one to craft expectations that account for their particular strengths and capabilities. Ideally, these individual goals should push them to achieve at a level slightly higher than the one at which they're already performing. You may have heard these called "stretch goals" because they make the person stretch a bit to reach them. They're designed for excellence, rather than averageness.

Let me say, first of all, that this isn't a formal process. I don't sit down with firefighters in turn and say, "Okay, you get my average expectations," "You get my gold-star expectations," and so forth. At least, it's not formal on their end. From my perspective, it's very formal, very deliberate. I know exactly what I expect of each of my officers. When I ran a company, I knew what I expected of each of my firefighters. And they knew, too, because during training, I would push the stars a little harder. The guys studying for lieutenant, the ones who really had it in them to be great officers, I pushed a little more. Simply by spending more time with them, I put the pressure on. By coaching them, I let them know that good enough really wasn't good enough. If it was, I wouldn't waste my time. They knew that, and they stepped up accordingly.

I had a young lieutenant once who had been promoted from a very quiet firehouse. Even though he'd passed the Test and earned his rank, he really didn't have a lot of experience—and frankly, it showed. Now, it was my job to help this young lieutenant raise the level of his performance to the point where he could actually be an asset to the department, because then, at the moment, he was not an asset. So what I started doing is, whenever he'd make a mistake, I'd pull him aside and explain what he'd done wrong and how to do it right the next time. At the same time, however, I'd let him know that so far, he wasn't doing the work I expected from an FDNY officer.

Now, I'm not a bully. I don't get off on making people nervous. But if I'd been happy-go-lucky about it, telling him, "Hey, come on into the office, have a cup of coffee. Don't worry about those leadership problems, it'll work itself out," do you think he would have improved? Of course not. But by letting him know what I expected of him, I generated a little creative anxiety. And he worked hard to relieve that anxiety. He kept at it until he was able to consistently meet my expectations.

That story may not be the stuff of leadership legends, but it proves my point. And ultimately, when that lieutenant finally moved on to another company, he came to me and thanked me for helping him become a more successful officer.

Expectations work their magic by raising the bar a little, which for most people results in stress. Up to a certain level, stress actually raises your performance. It focuses your thoughts, increases your energy, and clears your mind of distractions. Even high achievers feel stress when presented with stretch goals; their secret is that they put that stress to work and use it as fuel to get themselves to the next level.

In fact, a 1992 study of urban firefighters showed that the performance of experienced fire officers actually improved with stress. Of course, that study was focusing on environmental stress—the stress of battle, of firefighting—but practically speaking, it's the same thing with expectation-related stress.

But while stress, much like fire, is beneficial and even essential in small amounts, it can be a real problem if it gets out of hand. Too much stress leads to panic, smothers your ability to reason, and causes you to fall back on impulse and instinct, things that can actually interfere with your ability to effectively deal with whatever's going on. Stress also affects different people in different ways: what would be a crippling amount of stress for some is just a pleasant little jolt for another, which is why it's so important to tailor your expectations to the individual instead of relying on these clumsy, groupwide standards.

The more accurately you can calibrate your expectations to each person's specific needs and capabilities, the more likely that the result will be higher levels of performance.

In addition to tailoring expectations to your people, you need to be realistic. Don't expect the impossible; this only frustrates and demoralizes. You also need to be aware of how much of your people's performance rests on things beyond their control. As much as you can, try to come up with expectations that aren't going to be influenced by outside factors or dumb luck. At the end of the day, you want to be able to look at each person's achievements in as pure a light as possible.

Now, I know that some companies are letting their people set their own expectations. I know what you're thinking: Yeah right, like that's going to work. No matter how aligned your people are with the organization, or energized by the prospect of recognition or development opportunities, it's the rare person who's going to volunteer for tougher standards, year after year. On the other hand, don't you build accountability by letting people participate in the processes that concern them? If that's the case, then what's the solution here? Do you set expectations unilaterally, and risk alienating your people and undoing all the trust you've cultivated? Or do you let them somehow set their own bar and hope for the best?

Unfortunately, there's no simple answer to those questions. Leadership is an art, not a science. Leadership is not neat or tidy. Ultimately, you'll have to develop a unique approach to each case because each case—each person—is unique. All I can do is pass on what I've learned, which is this: you need to at least offer your people the *chance* to participate in setting expectations.

Listen to their rationale and incorporate their suggestions wherever appropriate. The more you listen to their input and act on it, the more they'll be inclined to commit, *really* commit, to the expectations. Giving people ownership creates a situation where they have a stake in things. Don't misunderstand: it's your job as the leader to establish standards. You're only consulting with your people, not throwing your authority over to them. But the more you can create a consultative atmosphere, the more likely people will be to summon up the intensity and drive so necessary for effective execution.

Working with your people to set expectations does result in higher levels of performance, but not by itself. The next leadership rung we'll look at may surprise you, but don't underestimate it. After all, optimism has always been the successful leader's secret weapon.

THE SECOND RUNG: EXHIBIT OPTIMISM

Things happen when you're fighting a fire that can instantly unnerve and demoralize your people. Ceilings collapse behind you, shutting you up inside an inferno. You run out of oxygen while searching for victims on the smoke-flooded floors above the fire. A member of your team takes a cautious step forward and disappears as the floor disappears beneath him. At moments like these, success—survival, even—seems very far away. And of course, there's no time to gather your men for a pep talk. All you can do is stay calm. Remember, the men are always watching. If they see you're not shaken by what's happening, but continue to act as if success is inevitable, then you relieve them of the need to worry and enable them to get on with doing their job. Staying calm under pressure is basically just operational optimism.

That's right. Optimism is another thing that makes great performance possible. If your people stay positive in the face of challenges and obstacles, they'll be more likely to overcome them than if they're hobbled by negativity or pessimism. To some of you, this may sound— I don't know, too touchy-feely, maybe. But remember: the mood of the group has a measurable impact on its success. Would you shrug at some new technology or process that offered you a leg up on the com-

petition? Of course not. It's your duty as a leader to embrace any competitive advantage you come across. And that's how you should think
of optimism: as a secret weapon, a competitive edge, that will help you
execute more swiftly than other organizations in your field.

Now, don't confuse optimism with the kind of self-delusion that
comes from an unwillingness to face up to reality. There's nothing
more depressing than watching a once-proud organization slide into
obsolescence, all the while insisting that it's a pioneer and a market
leader. That isn't optimism. That's fear, plus an inability to commit to
uncovering reality. However, like most aspects of leadership, optimism becomes really useful only when combined with other approaches. Assuming that you've uncovered the reality of a situation,
assessed your strengths, weaknesses, and true chance of success, and
crafted a credible operational plan—in other words, if you've prepared for execution—then optimism is that extra something that will
put you over the top.

Optimism makes a difference because it transforms attitudes and
beliefs about what's possible. It sounds corny, I know, but what your
people *believe* they're capable of is often more important than what
they're *actually* capable of. In this way, optimism acts as a kind of faith.
And like faith, optimism frees people from worry and anxiety, allowing them to focus on the matter at hand. It clears the mind of doubt,
and doubt is something that depresses your people's ability to operate
at full power. Because optimism assumes a positive future, it actually
makes your people more alert to new possibilities and opportunities.

There are several ways you can convey optimism to your people.
You can be generally upbeat, projecting a positive attitude, encouraging your people, and letting them know when they're doing a good
job. During times of change or turmoil, when people are naturally
uncertain and anxious, you can go out among your people and talk to
them about what's going on, making it clear that you're confident in
the group's chance of success. This approach also works when people

are having a tough time with a particular project or goal. But there's also another, quieter form of optimism, which we often get the opportunity to practice at the fire ground, and that's staying calm under pressure.

So now we've covered two of the steps necessary to enable your people to work effectively. You've learned about the importance of setting goals tailored to the individual, and the power of optimism. Next, you're going to discover the single most important factor in leading for high performance and results.

THE THIRD RUNG:
UNLEASH YOUR PEOPLE'S STRENGTHS

Sometimes your people aren't effective because you won't let them be. If it sounds like I'm accusing you of holding them back, I am. Remember the commitment to treating your people as assets? Well, too many leaders treat their people as liabilities instead. Would you ever try to force an auto plant to turn out refrigerators instead? Would you buy a word processing program and then try to use it as a spreadsheet? Of course not. And yet in organizations across the world, managers seem intent on misusing their most important assets, their people. They seem hell-bent on keeping their people in positions where they can't make the best use of their strengths, and this, of course, just limits everyone's ability to be effective and produce great results.

At this point, I think it might be helpful for everyone if I try and define exactly what I'm talking about when I refer to your people's "strengths." Strengths are not skills. They are not things that can be learned, or reduced to a one-size-fits-all series of steps. Instead, strengths are personal attributes or ways of being. They're vague, qualitative, and sometimes hard to put your finger on, which is probably why we try to ignore them. They don't necessarily show up in test scores or résumés; they're irritating that way.

But whenever you've described someone as being "good at" something—like computers, or fixing cars, or making small talk—you've touched on something that relates to his or her strengths. While a minimal level of competence can be learned in any of these areas, mastery is impossible without that unique mix of personality, experience, and aptitude that all strengths are made of. Strengths encompass such intangibles as empathy, attention to detail, the ability to make sense of apparently disconnected bits of information, a talent for relationship building, and a drive to succeed.

We have several strengths we look for in the FDNY, but the most important is a guy who's into the job. "Into the job" is an attitude, an intensity, a way of approaching your work. When you're into the job you're fully engaged. You're always trying to get experience with the latest tools and tactics. When you hear there's a second alarm in Queens, then even though you're in the Bronx, you turn on the radio to follow the operation as it unfolds. This attitude is what all great firefighters have in common. You can't teach it; it's one of those intangibles, the kind of strength you need to uncover during the interview process. I'd rather have a guy who's into the job, and maybe not quite so experienced, than someone with twenty years who's just going through the motions.

You can teach people how to do something, like how to program a VCR or devise a budget, but you can't teach them how to be *good at* something, like how to be good at making relationships, or at making intuitive leaps of reason. By trying to teach or train people to be good at something, to develop a strength that isn't already there, you're just setting them up for failure. So instead, focus on helping them use their strengths, and teach them to sidestep their weaknesses. Any other approach will waste their time, fritter away their confidence, and make them that much less effective.

If you're still skeptical about the whole notion of strengths, then consider all the times you've worked with people who, despite having similar intelligence, experience, and skills, performed at vastly different levels. What accounts for the differences in their effectiveness? Well, after you've isolated all their measurable qualities (experience, education, and so forth), all you're left with is their strengths. So the key to leading for execution is to identify—and help your people develop—their strengths, and then put them in positions where their strengths will be useful.

It's because I think it's so important that you be able to identify what your people are good at that I've advocated that you keep in constant contact with your employees. I haven't prescribed all this walking around and asking questions and observing because I'm a psychoanalyst trapped in a firefighter's body. It's just that it's really the only way to get a handle on what your people can do. Once you identify their strengths, then you can use teaching and coaching approaches as well as stretch goals to help them develop these qualities. Part of developing your people's strengths, however, is making sure they're in a position to use them in the first place.

The point of doing all this is not to make excuses for your underperformers, but to help you uncover their strengths, determine if their current job really draws on those strengths, and if not, match them to a position that will allow them to be useful. So to pull this off, you not only have to get to know your people; you also need to be familiar with the requirements of other positions in your organization. By disciplining yourself to uncover and define the true needs of each job, you'll soon develop a sense of the qualities needed to succeed in these various roles.

We've now covered three of the rungs on our climb to an execution culture: setting performance goals, optimism, and discovering your people's strengths. But the question now is, how do you get your people to use those strengths to do meaningful work?

THE FOURTH RUNG: ALLOW EXECUTION

It's not enough to select the right people, deploy them so that they can use their strengths, and then try to keep them in positions where they can be effective. The most important part of leading for execution is simply letting your people execute in the first place. One of the first runs we had after I took command of 48 Engine in the Bronx was for a fire in a taxpayer, a building containing a row of stores. Our firefighting procedures call for stretching a two-and-a-half-inch hose to these types of buildings, and I wanted to make sure my guys pulled the right line off the rig. As I turned to give the order for a two-and-a-half, I saw my guys already pulling hose down the sidewalk toward me where I was standing in front of the building. It was a two-and-a-half-inch hose.

I can't take credit for their actions, because I had just arrived in the company, but it was obvious to me that I had a company with dedicated firefighters who had the knowledge and training to do their jobs without my making every decision for them. They were good and they knew it. And now I did too.

This story takes us back to the commitment to use your people as assets. Of course, you wouldn't acquire an asset that was designed to perform a certain function in a particular way, and then try to change the way it works. Not if you wanted it to work effectively (or at all). And your people—your true assets—are no different. You've made it possible for them to make their strengths useful; now you need to give them the freedom to decide how to use those strengths to achieve the desired outcomes. You've got to give them the breathing space to be great on their own terms.

Empowerment is an old story in the FDNY. While we do employ a command-and-control structure, we couldn't possibly maintain our high levels of effectiveness if we didn't trust our people to get the job done. There's simply no time for micromanaging when you're operating in an emergency situation. You may have people trapped in a collapse, you may have fire jumping to another building, there could be toxic fumes or hazardous chemicals involved, and on top of that you're responsible for deploying and managing between twenty-four and a hundred men. You really don't have time to wander over to whoever has the pipe (*pipe* is slang for the hose's nozzle) and say, "You know, I think you should be aiming that over *there*." Or to a truckie, "Vent *this* window first."

It's because of our people that we're the best at what we do. We manage by communicating objectives to them and then giving them the freedom to reach those objectives according to their own strengths and instincts. Obviously, we couldn't do this if we didn't thoroughly train our people and make sure they understood the basic guidelines of our operation. We don't take probies fresh from the academy and tell them, "Hey, tiger, go knock down that third-floor blaze for me." But for the most part, we treat our people as the experienced professionals that they are. Pride is part of what motivates them, pride in their craft and accomplishments; we're not about to take that away by telling them how to do their jobs.

Of course, it's natural to want to exert some control over how your people do things. After all, you've got a lot of useful experience, and insight into how things work, and the heat is on you to get things done, not to give your people time to experiment and tinker. Right? Well, yes and no. You do have lots of useful experience and insight, but you should use these as teaching tools, not as templates for the "right way" to do things. And yes, the heat is on you to get things done, but forcing your people to conform to a particular approach will bring only predictability, not performance. By telling your people how they should do things, you smother the breakthroughs, innovations, and valuable shortcuts that come when you let people find their own way.

This is not a revolutionary idea. Sociologists have discovered that even across widely diverse cultures, people want the freedom to exercise choice, assert their own identity, and achieve respect and dignity.

You empower your people when you permit them to chart their own course to achievement. But you also allow them to take responsibility for the results, a responsibility that naturally leads to ownership, accountability, and commitment.

In addition to making it impossible for your people to use their strengths, by telling them how to do everything you imply that you have no confidence in their abilities. It's demeaning for your people to be told that they can't be trusted to get things done. Take away your people's chance to be successful on their own terms and you also siphon off their enthusiasm and initiative. This also makes you central to the execution process; doesn't really sound like a recipe for efficiency, right? Your people will need to come to you for direction in every little thing. They're following *your* plan, after all; their own initiative is useless. Treat them as mindless, ineffectual drones, and they'll have no choice but to lower themselves to meet your expectations.

There's a difference, however, between empowerment and neglect. Some leaders talk about throwing their people into the deep end and letting them learn to swim. I'm not sure this is that great an approach. Granted, your people will probably learn not to drown, but not drowning doesn't always mean doing the Australian crawl. Give your people the opportunity to blaze their own trails, but let them know you're standing by to help them out if they need it. It's important that you know how to support your people as they take some chances and find new and better ways to accomplish their goals.

Make Sure Their Objectives Are Clear

We covered this in the chapter on execution, but it's worth repeating: be sure that your people understand exactly what they should be trying to achieve. Illustrate the desired outcomes as precisely as possible. Discuss with your people how their work toward this objective helps out with the organization's long-term goals, and how it relates to creating value for the customer. In short, make sure they know exactly where they're going before they start figuring out how to get there.

Believe in Them

I know, I know—am I a therapist, or a leader? But get over it. Just as your people are influenced by your moods and behaviors, you also have a lot of power over how they see themselves. You have to show them that you believe they'll succeed in their endeavors. You have to act as if you just assume they'll be able to get it done—they're so good you have no doubt they'll succeed. Let people know that you believe in them, and they'll work doubly hard to meet your expectations and justify your faith in their abilities.

Encourage Risk Taking, Accept Mistakes

Part of the reason for letting your workers do things their way is that experimentation and innovation often result. Because you haven't told them of a right way to do things, they'll make their own way, which sometimes ends up being more effective. But as you know, this sort of experimentation doesn't work without the freedom to take risks and make mistakes. So don't merely tolerate risk taking, make sure people know it's a good thing. Instead of jumping all over your employees for the honest mistakes they make while trying to get results, use those mistakes as teaching and coaching opportunities. Mistakes are your people's best chance to grow, and the only unforgivable mistakes are the ones that are made twice.

Keep Yourself in the Loop

Keep in the loop through the milestones and progress reports we discussed in the last two chapters. These processes give your people the opportunity to fill you in on what's happening, ask questions, and give you the heads-up on problems or mistakes that they need help with. They're also a reminder of your presence, proof that you're standing by and available whenever your people feel they're in over their heads.

When you try to impose your own way of doing things on your people, you actually just distract them from getting things done. Now they have to focus not on getting results but on doing things *your* way. This is why, sometimes, leading for execution means knowing when to get out of the way. But you've still got to stay in the picture. It's a tough balancing act. So given everything you've just learned, how do you serve as a resource for your people?

THE FIFTH RUNG: GIVE FEEDBACK

Ed Koch, former mayor of New York City, used to ask voters, "How'm I doing?" Now, Koch was responsible for the infamous Super Bowl Sunday firehouse closing. What happened was, on the day of the Super Bowl, firefighters from 232 Engine were sent out on a run, only to discover that not only was there no fire to contain, but their firehouse was at that very moment being boarded up and their company disbanded. So in light of this, I have an idea of how I might have answered his question. But regardless of how I felt about him, by asking that question the mayor was simply doing something you have to do in order to be effective: he was looking for feedback.

Feedback means letting your people know how they're doing. This includes both critiquing their efforts and recognizing their triumphs. Without some kind of objective analysis of their progress, your people will have no idea how they're doing. Are they making progress? Are they way off track? Deny them the benefit of these observations, and you not only make it impossible for them to figure out how they could improve, but take away their chance for growth and development.

But some leaders don't want to play this role. Why? Because in order for it to be worthwhile, any discussion you have with your people about their performance has to be completely honest. That means you'll have to tell them about some unpleasant things, like their weaknesses, failures, and shortcomings. Leaders who avoid candid discussions with their employees about their performance don't do it because they're afraid of hurting their people's feelings, but because they don't want to face the fact that they're responsible for their people's development.

Feedback alone, however, isn't enough to spark improvement. You need to be able to offer the person a practical plan for overcoming his weaknesses at the same time that you're outlining his shortcomings. If you have no idea how he can improve his performance, hold off on your feedback until you figure it out. Anytime someone receives criticism, it throws him off balance and makes him vulnerable; or if you want to look at it another way, it makes him particularly receptive to your teaching. If you can combine feedback with a plan for positive action, you can capture his disappointment and channel it into productive energy.

The evil twin of the leader who can't give honest feedback about her people's areas of weakness is the one who can't seem to offer praise or recognition. This leader, far from being concerned about appearing too harsh, actually thinks that by praising her people she'll make them soft, or perhaps that they don't need praise, because, after all, they're just doing what they're paid to do, right? But as we've already seen, money is not one of the things that motivates people. Recognition, respect, the sense that their contribution has been acknowledged or valued—these are what people crave.

For example, my friend Marty Monaghan and his company—his is captain of 36 Ladder in the Inwood section of Manhattan—were awarded a unit citation for their role in fighting a serious fire in that area. This "unit," as we call the award, was a huge moral booster, not just for the six men on that tour, but for every firefighter in the company. It raised the company's level of pride and self-worth, and from what Marty tells me, left them eager to exceed the already high level at which they operated.

After every operation, I try to recognize my firefighters' efforts and let them know I appreciate all the hard work. And if I think they've done a great job, an extraordinary job, the department has created more formal kinds of recognition. For example, we have unit citations that we use to acknowledge outstanding companies. These are probably my favorites, since they enable us to call attention to superior levels of teamwork and coordination, things I want all our people to aspire to. And of course, we recognize individual acts of heroism as well. The highest award in the department, the James Gordon Bennett Medal, is awarded each year to the firefighter who has exhibited the greatest bravery in executing his mission.

Recognition and praise are the most effective, least expensive ways to motivate people. It's easy to forget, as a leader, just how much weight your opinion carries with your people. And even if you're aware of your negative power (for example, your people don't like it when you yell at them), you can still be oblivious to your positive power, that is, your praise, which is equally meaningful. And on top of that, it doesn't cost you a thing. I mean, I've got a whole drawer full of "Thank you's" and "good job's."

It's very easy, I think, for managers to fall into the trap of focusing on the people who seem to be having the most trouble. But don't forget what we talked about in terms of putting your resources where you'll get the most out of them. You should actually spend more time working with your best people. Even though it seems that they need it less than anyone else—I mean, look at what a great job they're already doing!—this is all the more reason you should be focusing on them. Think how amazing they'll be once you really start working with them to isolate and work around their weak spots. And don't underestimate the degree to which your top people are motivated by praise and recognition; the last thing you want is for them to slacken their efforts because they think they're unappreciated or ignored.

Unfortunately, some leaders still treat the feedback process as part of the standard, once-a-year performance review. The best way to ensure that you take the time to give your people useful feedback is to make it a part of your leadership routine. You're already meeting with your people to discuss their progress toward their various milestones; take that opportunity to give them feedback on their overall progress as well. As always, discuss their strengths and weaknesses in the context of their position's requirements, their individual goals, and also the overall, big-picture stuff about the organization's mission and customers.

By now it should be starting to come together. You can see how the commitments, the emphasis on connecting with your people, trust, and decision making all facilitate execution. But how do you sustain execution? How do you make sure people continue to get things done over the long term?

THE SIXTH RUNG: HELP YOUR PEOPLE IMPROVE

The FDNY has always been committed to finding new ways to help its people grow and develop. Even before 1883, when Assistant Chief Hugh Bonner created the School of Instruction on the third floor of Engine Company 47's Amsterdam Avenue firehouse, the company officers and senior men would train and drill their firefighters daily. Today, that ongoing commitment to development has given birth to the Fire Academy, a twenty-seven-acre campus on Randall's Island. There are several ongoing programs at the academy, aimed at firefighters of all ranks, from probie to chief officer. There are fire and smoke simulators, management courses, a haz-mat training site, and a civil defense center. In fact, firefighters come to the academy from all over the country to learn the latest firefighting strategies and techniques.

But we also know that helping our people grow goes beyond supervised training. There are all kinds of special projects and assignments we use as development tools; and of course, for motivated firefighters (which is most of them), there's also the option of transferring into a different kind of company—one of the elite units, or a busier house, or one situated in a different environment (say, the brownstones of Brooklyn rather than the skyscrapers of Midtown Manhattan).

The most interesting—and meaningful, as far as my own development was concerned—of the special projects I've been involved with came along a few years ago, when I was still a captain. At the time, the department believed that we needed to overhaul the training program for basic engine company tactics. The inspiration for this change was a series of deaths—I believe it was eleven men over a two-year period—that convinced the department that the existing curriculum wasn't really preparing firefighters for the changing nature of the job. Basically, the training then was outdated. And I was asked to design and develop the new curriculum, which was really a great opportunity for me.

I recruited a handful of officers for the project team, and together we created the whole program from the ground up. The process of transforming what I had learned as both a firefighter and an officer into material that anyone could absorb and make use of really helped me to become a more effective teacher once I returned to my duties as a company officer. The project also allowed me to put my strengths to work in a new area and feel the pride of accomplishment that comes from mastering something challenging and unfamiliar. You know, eleven thousand firefighters went through that program, the program I helped create. This was not only a growth experience; it allowed me to see a different side of what had become a familiar job. It challenged me and helped me develop. As a result, I returned to my command reenergized and motivated.

Leaders need to focus on doing better each day than they did the day before. Continuous improvement is the key to keeping up those high levels of performance. In a way, the final component of execution is preparing your people to achieve goals that are still waiting to be defined: in other words, preparing them for the future. For a leader, this means focusing on developing your people and making sure they have access to new training and opportunities, because the only sure thing in today's world is that your operating environment will become more competitive, challenging, and unforgiving. Complacency is the real enemy of long-term effectiveness. If your people aren't ready for the future, then neither is your organization.

It shouldn't come as a surprise that the best opportunities for growth and development take place outside the classroom. In fact, studies have found that 80 percent of all learning takes place without anyone ever lifting a no. 2 pencil. With this in mind, try to create development opportunities that live in the real world. Devise new projects and positions that allow your people to wrestle with cutting-edge challenges and technologies, or scout out new opportunities for the organization. Make it possible for employees to transfer into other positions or areas of the organization, and experiment with new roles that will challenge them to develop their strengths in different ways. Circulating your employees through different roles and special teams will allow you to spread new ways of doing things throughout your group or organization.

But helping people grow through new experiences is only one way of tending to their development. You can also study other organizations and look for innovations that help them get things done more effectively. If you want to spread these best practices through your own group, then start by assembling a small team of unofficial leaders from each level of your unit, teach them the new approach, and then make them accountable for sharing it with their colleagues. You can also try rotating your employees through a series of workshops designed to teach them the new process.

While you might think that the most obvious place to look for best practices is among your competitors, other valuable resources include your best and brightest (often, your top people will be innovating some fantastic new stuff right under your nose), as well as the leading organizations in other fields. Jack Welch was inspired to adopt Six Sigma, a quality-assurance process, after seeing the results Motorola had achieved with it. The FDNY, when it first became a professional organization, borrowed liberally from the military's organizational strategy. Beneath the apparent differences in product, customer, and industry, organizations are all engaged in the same basic activity: creating value through their employees. But how can you suss out these best practices? Well, it's the same old story, I'm afraid: by reading, embracing new experiences, and being open to learning from a variety of sources.

Finally, the expectations we discussed as part of the first rung play an important role in your people's development. Work with them to devise performance standards that will push them to keep developing their strengths. These kinds of standards will stimulate your people to work the next level, and when coupled with some of the other approaches we've covered here, will mean more effective execution over the long haul.

In previous chapters we looked at what execution is. We sharpened our understanding of how things get done. We saw how the way we follow through on decisions either supports or undermines our ability to succeed.

In this chapter, I showed you the six specific things you need to do to make your people the main drivers of an execution culture. I likened these six things to the rungs of a ladder, one you climb to reach your ultimate goal, which is personal accountability. In fact, this is what we've been aiming for all along. Once your people hold themselves accountable for their performance, then you can really start to accomplish some amazing things as a leader.

Now let's move on to chapter 10 and study how smart leaders use change and innovation as opportunities to develop high-performing organizations.

Straight from the Chief

The essence of leading for execution lies in guiding an organization or a group of people so that they not only get things done but get the right things done. There are six rungs on this ladder, but in the end the most important thing you can do is give your people the chance to use their strengths to accomplish their goals; this will make them feel successful, and making people feel that they have the chance to be successful is the key to motivating them to get the right things done.

1. **Establish clear expectations.** Setting specific and realistic expectations will inspire people to raise their level of performance.
2. **Instill optimism.** Confident leadership is proven to help people overcome obstacles and work more effectively.
3. **Put people in a position to use their strengths.** Discover what your people are good at, and put them in roles where they can draw on these strengths.
4. **Let them do things their way.** When you let people achieve objectives in their own way, they'll reward your faith in them with innovative solutions and energetic execution.
5. **Provide feedback.** Constantly update people on their progress and offer them constructive criticism if necessary. People won't know how they're really doing unless you tell them. This also means praising them if they're doing a great job!
6. **Foster continuous improvement.** This is the key to a successful organization. When you expose your people to new experiences and help them learn new skills, you make possible the fresh ideas and insights that will help your company thrive.

CHAPTER 10

The Fire You Beat Today
Is Not the One You'll Face Tomorrow

How do you make uncertainty and flux
work to your advantage?

Organizations might as well be alive. Just like any other organisms, they compete with one another for resources, develop different strategies to help them foil predators, and fight to defend their niche in the ecosystem. And also like other living things, organizations must evolve and adapt to changes in their environments or they'll become extinct. I've got five kids, so you know I've been to the Museum of Natural History about a million times. My kids loved the dinosaur bones, but for me they're a reminder of how quickly you can be wiped out by changes in your environment.

To help your organization survive change, you need to innovate. Every good leader is part entrepreneur, always on the lookout for new ways to create value for his customers. Every good leader is also part bellwether, watching for and helping his organization survive the inevitable shifts in its natural habitat. He does this not only by recognizing when change is needed but also by knowing when to initiate it and how to manage it.

This is exactly what Chief Engineer Edward Croker was doing in the early 1900s when he pressed city politicians and businesspeople for more comprehensive fire safety regulations, including mandatory automatic sprinklers and alarms. Croker's New York City was more brutal than the metropolis we know today. In its rush to grow, the city had become remarkably contemptuous of its citizens' safety. Buildings were rising well beyond the reach of the fire department's ladders. Offices and factories made no provisions for the safety of their inhabitants. Business responsibility was an unknown concept. In fact, the city's business community was so opposed to Croker's propositions that its members began spreading rumors that his call for automatic sprinklers was nothing more than a payoff to a sprinkler company.

Croker also urged the city to give him the funds to create a specialized bureau of the FDNY dedicated to fire prevention. As he envisioned it, this new bureau would have the power to inspect any building, at any time, and compel the owner to make fire safety improvements if necessary. Though they may not seem so today, all of Croker's initiatives were innovations. Conceived of as new ways of preserving the lives of New York's citizens (which, as I mentioned earlier, is the primary mission of the FDNY and the value we provide to our "customers"), these initiatives were every bit as innovative as the more obvious advances in fire suppression—the steam-powered apparatus, for instance—if not more so. But despite the obvious benefits of Croker's proposals, he was ignored and even persecuted for trying to be a responsible leader.

All that changed on March 25, 1911. That was the day fire ripped through the Triangle Shirtwaist Company. The Triangle Shirtwaist Company was a light-industry operation employing six hundred people. It occupied the top three floors of the ten-story Asch Building, near Washington Square in Greenwich Village. Contained within those three floors were hundreds of yards of fabric waiting to be stitched into merchandise by young women who sat obediently, row after row, behind their sewing machines for hours at a time.

The Asch Building was fireproof, but its contents and inhabitants were anything but. The building had no exterior fire escapes, and the doors of the one interior escape stairway were kept locked to stop employees from taking unscheduled breaks.

The fire broke out at four-forty in the afternoon. The first engine company arrived about six minutes later, but the flames had already stormed through all three floors. Smoke was melting from the windows in great black drags, and the bodies of young women who had jumped to escape the flames were strewn along the near edge of Greene Street. As the firefighters arrived, more panicked faces appeared at the windows. The firefighters brought out their new life nets, but the nets weren't designed to contain the energy that a body accumulates during a hundred-foot fall, and they ruptured from the force of the impacts. Onlookers reported that those who jumped often did so in groups of three or four.

A young firefighter from Engine Company 18 reported that the first thing he saw upon arriving at the Asch Building "was a man's body come crashing down. . . . We turned into Greene Street and began to stretch in our hoses. The bodies were hitting all around us."

The department's tallest ladders reached only to the sixth floor, and by the time the firefighters deployed their scaling ladders—another new innovation, a kind of portable ladder designed to be raised one floor at a time, window to window, on a building's exterior—it was all over: 146 people were dead. The city coroner, no stranger to corpses and calamity, wept as he examined the ruined bodies. Firefighters tenderly drew the dead ladies from a hole in the asphalt created by their violent impact. Croker surveyed the human wreckage, both at street level and in the incinerated company offices. He was furious. The Triangle Shirtwaist tragedy was exactly the kind of pointless disaster his initiatives had been designed to avoid.

In the end, the Triangle Shirtwaist tragedy was the price the city had to pay to get Croker's innovations adopted. Outraged citizens and sympathetic politicians took up the fire chief's cause, and the next year the FDNY was given the authority to create a powerful Bureau of Fire Prevention, which wasted no time in embarking on a widespread campaign of building inspections—more than a hundred thousand in the first year. In addition, the fire commissioner was granted the power to condemn buildings with insufficient fire safety measures. In retrospect, there's no doubt that Croker's innovations—and those of the fire chiefs before him who had lobbied for similar changes—have saved more lives than all the heroic sacrifices firefighters have made throughout the organization's history.

Although people seem to use the words interchangeably, *innovation* and *change* don't mean the same thing. Innovation is something you choose to do; you seek it out as a means of growing and strengthening your business. For example, the fire pole was an innovation, devised in 1888, to enable firefighters to respond to alarms more quickly. On the other hand, the transition from an all-volunteer firefighting force to a professional organization was a change necessitated by shifts in the nature of the job itself. Thus, change is usually a response to something that's happening in your environment. It's pushed on you. While there's certainly a lot of overlap between the two—sometimes to survive change you need to innovate, or an innovation will lead to an industry-wide need for change—the basic distinction remains: innovation is a choice, while change is an imperative.

Of course, your organization's survival is not threatened by a fire (hopefully). Instead, it's new economic trends, social developments, technologies, and discoveries. Change might show up as a better product or service, or a shift in what your customer values, or new rules or regulations that make it impossible for you to keep going along as you used to. But ironically, while change carries with it the possibility of an organization's extinction, it's also a great opportunity for growth and improvement. In fact, the basis of most innovation is a change of one kind or another.

So here's the short version: leaders must master both innovation and change to be effective. The first is a powerful driver of growth, while the second is essential to your organization's survival.

WHAT, EXACTLY, IS INNOVATION?

Innovation is really about value. When you innovate, you provide value for your customers in new ways, through a new product, a lower price, a fresh convenience, the creation of a new desire, or a product or service that leads to a new kind of customer satisfaction. Innovations can also help you to continue providing an existing value more effectively or profitably.

The one thing all those kinds of innovation have in common is their focus on creating some new value for the customer. And that's certainly been the case in the FDNY. Each of our innovations has contributed to a safer city. For example, in the early 1850s, we had Chief Alfred Carson connecting the city's bell towers (essentially, towers manned by a lookout who watched for signs of fire) to department headquarters by telegraph. Chief John Bresnan, an influential leader from the late 1800s, has several innovations to his credit, including the fire pole and a special nozzle designed for close-quarters use, as in a cellar, that we still carry today. It's called a Bresnan distributor. Another tool, probably the defining instrument of our profession, the Halligan tool, was also named for its fire chief inventor. A kind of crowbar topped with a stubby axe head, the Halligan tool was designed fifty years ago and has yet to be improved on. Another innovation, of course, was Chief Croker's Bureau of Fire Prevention; and even before him, Chief Bresnan and his colleague Chief Hugh Bonner were instrumental in pushing through new fire safety codes for New York City's overcrowded tenements. And this is just a slender accounting of all the insightful, even revolutionary ideas that have come out of the FDNY.

Usually, when you hear about innovations, you get the idea that it's some kind of magical process. Innovators themselves are portrayed as creative powerhouses able to tune in to a special frequency where new ideas are theirs for the taking. But these are really just fairy tales. Real innovation consists mainly of hard work and discipline. That's not all, of course: talent, ingenuity, and the right attitude play their parts. You also need to adopt and stick to a system that will help you uncover new opportunities for innovation. But overall it's the disciplined, persistent labor of the committed entrepreneur that makes innovation possible.

HOW CAN I BECOME MORE INNOVATIVE?

It's no secret that one of the largest areas of concern within the FDNY is the quality of our incident communications system, by which I mean the radio system that incident commanders use to maintain contact with their people. We'd always been aware of the uneven quality of the radio system and had tried several different solutions, but none of them really solved the problem. The radios continued to fail in certain situations, such as fires in high-rise buildings that made it necessary for us to operate in subways or underground conduits. However, it wasn't until September 11 that we understood just how catastrophic a communications failure could be. In the aftermath of that operation, while we were reviewing what had happened, it became clear that both internal FDNY and interagency (FDNY to NYPD, to FEMA, and so forth) radio communication problems had sharply undermined our effectiveness.

But even though 9/11 confirmed with horrific authority just how badly we needed improved communications equipment, none of the companies we worked with seemed able to solve the problem. Of course, in the end, all it took was an FDNY captain, on duty with our research and development unit, to come up with the answer. His solution was a portable twenty-five-watt booster unit that would enable an officer to maintain contact with his firefighters in just about any environment. In effect, the booster unit transforms the officer carrying it into a central communications clearinghouse. With this system, you could have a booster unit at the command post in the lobby of a high-rise, with enough power to transmit to a secondary command post higher up in the building. The officer at the secondary post would have a unit as well, with which he could reach all the firefighters working throughout the building.

This captain, using nothing more than an electronics degree and some spare parts, fashioned a prototype, which the FNDY tested (successfully) before contracting for production models with some of the same multimillion-dollar companies that hadn't been able to innovate a solution on their own. So—not to gloat—this is a good example of how being close to the customer really gives you a unique insight into what they value and how best to capture that value through innovation.

One thing people don't always realize is that innovation happens only because of some kind of shortcoming in our existing ways of creating value. Innovation is how we respond to things like an unsatisfied need or a customer's new definition of value. In other words, innovation usually results in an improvement of some sort. Therefore, whenever you have room for improvement, you also have opportunities for innovation. Generally speaking, innovation starts in two places: change and value.

Change is great stuff. Really. It creates instability. It mixes up the relationships between ideas, people, and organizations. It leads to uncertainty. It's a little like a fire that way: you never know what it's going to do, but you know it's going to take away what was there before and leave something different when it's gone. And just as each stage of a fire creates different opportunities for fighting it, change creates different opportunities for innovation. In fact, one of my favorite little sayings is "Change is good." My men, I'm sure, probably find it kind of amusing that it comes out of my mouth so often, but I say it because it's true. When we have change we have an opportunity to create something new, something more efficient, safer, or easier.

The opposite of change is stability. When you have stability, you have very little opportunity to innovate. Everything is defined. There are no uncertainties, new possibilities, or unmet needs. But introduce even the slightest bit of change into this situation, and suddenly you'll see all kinds of opportunities opening up.

Value is the other key to innovation. The perfectly stable system I described above is, obviously, impossible. There are always unmet needs, gaps between the value that customers want and the value delivered by the organizations that serve those customers. By uncovering these shortcomings, you can craft innovative solutions that will satisfy the unmet needs of these customers.

Knowing that innovation exploits either change or value or both, you can develop a system that will help you identify areas that are ripe for innovation. Start by becoming more aware of change, specifically changes in your environment. Open yourself up to new, relevant sources of information. For example, you could resolve to read two new industry magazines or newsletters each month, go to a lecture or seminar, or read a book. Then, based on what you've learned, try to identify an emerging trend and think of an innovation that might take advantage of it. Write that idea down and put it in your innovation file. If you can, clip the magazine or newspaper article that inspired you and put it in there, too. Don't worry too much at first about whether or not your organization could use this new idea; the point of this exercise is to develop your muscles and get your mind used to seeing the world in terms of innovation opportunities.

Questioning why you're doing things a certain way or why you're using specific tactics or methods is a great way of staying ahead of the curve. Sometimes you may find that your organization is doing something in a certain way because "we've always done it this way." Question the original premise when examining these ideas and often you'll find that the entire process or procedure is based on a flawed or outdated proposition.

You can also discipline yourself to uncover your customers' unmet, unsatisfied needs. Hopefully this will be a little more familiar since it's basically the same as adopting an outside-in mind-set. To uncover areas where you can provide a new value to your customers, you just need to stay as close to them as possible. This means not only looking for situations where you can interact with them—for instance, you could go along on sales calls, or take advantage of focus groups, or save customers from burning buildings—but also tapping into your frontline people, the ones who work with your customers every day. Finally, don't forget that you can discover new ways of creating value by checking under your organization's hood for inconsistencies, bottlenecks, and other process inefficiencies, and improving them.

But whether you innovate based on value or change, the most important thing is that you be disciplined and consistent. The author Damon Knight, when asked where his ideas came from, said, "Everywhere. If you're looking for something *all the time,* no matter what it is, you'll find it." Follow Knight's advice and you'll soon find that once you begin looking for innovation, you'll discover all kinds of possibilities. But how do you tell the difference between a useful idea and an impractical daydream? It's a good question, and I've come up with three guidelines that will help you sort the wheat from the chaff:

- Innovations should be useful now.
- Innovations should provide a specific value to a specific customer.
- Innovations should be cheap.

Be Useful Now

While I know that I described innovation as something you do to ensure your organization's long-term survival, that doesn't mean innovations should be useful only in the distant future. Even if the full potential of an idea won't be realized for several years, it still needs to have some immediate benefit for your organization. Otherwise you may be throwing away valuable resources—money, people, and time—on a project that might never amount to anything.

However, the immediate benefit doesn't necessarily have to be a new product or service. Maybe the experience your people will get in developing this new idea will help them be more effective in their current jobs. Or maybe one of the near-future by-products of developing a new technology or approach can be used right away and represents an innovation for your organization in its own right. Maybe the growth and new expertise that you get from pursuing an innovation can be used to help your organization enter new markets.

Our squad companies are a fine example of this principle in action. While their main purpose is to expand our ability to manage hazardous-materials incidents, which Ray Downey and others anticipated would be a growing part of our job, the squads can also serve at fire operations and provide a level of support and special expertise similar to that of the elite rescue units. In other words, their haz-mat capabilities may not be called on every day, but in the meantime, the units still play a vital role in our fire and rescue operations.

Provide a Specific Value to a Specific Customer

Make your innovations as focused as possible. Know exactly what sort of value you're going to create with this new idea and also have a specific idea of who's going to appreciate this value. The idea here is to guard against those situations where you fall in love with a new piece of technology and rush it to market without first figuring out what value will be created and who will care.

One of the first questions I ask when a new procedure or piece of equipment is introduced is, "What problem is this solving?" I welcome new ideas and technologies, but only when they improve upon a situation or solve a problem. The last thing any organization needs is to spend time and money on things that don't deliver a benefit equal to their price tag or learning curve.

A most obvious example of companies that didn't seem to ask themselves this question would be the late-nineties rash of outfits offering products over the Internet, or integrating Internet technologies into their existing offerings, for no other reason than that they could and it seemed kind of cool. Did anyone stop to wonder if consumers really valued the ability to order toothpaste online?

Bootstrap Your Innovations Whenever Possible

Bootstrapping means doing things as cheaply and efficiently as you can. Diverting too many resources to an unproven idea is a risk that has a way of quickly cooling people's enthusiasm for a project. Even after you get the go-ahead from your superiors to implement an innovative idea, you're still on the bubble. Your project can be killed instantly, and usually will be if it seems like it's sucking more resources from the organization than it will be giving back anytime soon. Hiring too many people, spending extravagantly on new offices or equipment, or even promoting the project too eagerly once you get the go-ahead—in other words, doing anything to attract attention—will not help your cause.

The more people know about your project and the more room it takes up as a line item in the budget, the greater the chance it will go under the knife during the next budget crunch. So start small, stay focused, and do a lot with a little.

HOW CAN I LEAD FOR INNOVATION?

By teaching your people to be entrepreneurial, you improve your organization's prospects for growth. After all, if having one person in your group (you) innovating is a good thing, then having lots of people (your employees) doing so is even better. How well you're able to cultivate innovative attitudes in your people depends on how successful you've been in teaching them about the value your organization creates and how much freedom you've given them to accomplish objectives as they see fit.

Probably the worst thing you could do is just tell your people, "Be innovative." That's about as helpful as telling them to be better athletes or better nuclear physicists. Instead, you need to teach them *how* to innovate. Offer them examples of innovations that have been successful in your own organization or industry. Describe innovation in terms of outcomes; remember, you're looking for a new way of providing value to the customer. Recognize and praise examples of innovation, and then, while you have everyone's attention, explain why some idea or insight qualifies as such. It doesn't matter if these new ideas or innovations don't quite make the cut. It may take two or three or twenty attempts before someone hits on a successful concept. At the end of the day, what you're really trying to do is create a climate of risk taking and a willingness to think of new and better ways of doing the job.

Over the years, the FDNY has become very good at adapting to changes in its environment, mainly because our leaders have been so active in developing an internal culture of innovation. The sheer volume of meaningful innovation that has emerged from the ranks of firefighters, as well as the officer corps, shows that we've managed to cultivate an environment where fresh ideas can flourish. Simply by remaining open to our people's creativity and showing them—by adopting the innovations that truly make a difference—that we value their input, we've engaged our people's best selves. And the more a person feels she's contributing substantially to an endeavor, the more personally invested in it she'll become. It's this personal investment that leads people to work at ever higher levels of performance and effectiveness.

I was reminded of all this recently when I was puttering around in the kitchen of my Tremont Avenue firehouse. Not that our kitchen is all that innovative. Rather, it was the loud banging coming from somewhere beneath me that caught my attention. Following the noise to the basement, I discovered two welded, painted steel beams drilled into the floor and the ceiling, and between the beams, a metal door, the kind you'll find at the threshold of almost every apartment in New York. As I watched, a young firefighter approached the door and began forcing it open with his Halligan. I suddenly realized I was witnessing the maiden voyage of Battalion 18's very first homemade door-forcing simulator.

I wasn't surprised by what the men had done. And I knew that the inspiration for this device hadn't come to them in a dream or a vision or something. My company officers had spoken with their veteran firefighters about the large influx of young, inexperienced firefighters who had joined the department following 9/11, and they'd all agreed that they would have to be more creative and ingenious in their approach to training. Actual opportunities to perform forcible entry are necessarily limited to the number of locked or obstructed doors we encounter, so these resourceful firefighters had cooked up this simulator to help supplement the probies' education.

Not only had my men taken the initiative in innovating this very useful, rather ingenious new training device, but I knew they'd been pretty resourceful in going about it. There's not a lot of cash floating around the FDNY—you should see our furniture—and not only did they get a door manufacturer on Park Avenue in the Bronx to donate flawed or damaged doors that they could practice on, but I'm pretty sure they kicked in some of their own money to finish the job.

This is actually a pretty unremarkable story by department standards, but just because we've come to expect this sort of thing doesn't mean we don't understand how precious it is. We encourage this kind of behavior, first by always singling it out and praising it, and second, by telling other people about it. We'll tell officers in other firehouses, firefighters will tell other firefighters, guys will drop by to check it out for themselves, and the innovation will spread and may even become formally adopted as part of department policy. More important, as news of these innovations spreads, it reinforces the value of qualities like entrepreneurship and creativity, and raises the bar for innovation across the organization. Guys will hear about something firefighters in another house have done, and think, Hey, we can do better than that. And then to prove it, they'll go ahead and *do* something better.

Now, the guys who built the simulator didn't do it to get a pat on the head. They did it because they saw it would be valuable to them and help them accomplish their goals. So work on finding ways to plant that entrepreneurial spirit in your people. As I indicated earlier, you can discuss innovation during routine meetings. Talk to your people about the areas they should focus on, given their strengths, and press them to set goals in those areas. Follow up with them on these goals, and coach them as they try to uncover entrepreneurial opportunities. And remember to fortify your people's commitment to innovation: recognition and praise are still the most effective methods, but other rewards, like a day off, gift certificates, or even naming the new innovation after the employee, can also work wonders, if awarded promptly.

Innovation is really just the next logical step among the attitudes and approaches we've been discussing throughout this book. A commitment to following the smoke, an understanding of what your customers and organization value, and a focus on results are all key elements of an entrepreneurial outlook. But while innovation will help your organization grow by developing more effective ways to create value, sometimes only the ability to change will keep your organization alive.

CHANGE

Warren Bennis called change "the source of organizational salvation." While this is absolutely true, mismanaged change is also the source of a lot of organizational damnation. As a company's environment changes—for example, as customers rethink their definitions of value—in order to survive, an organization will need to change, as well, if it wants to be able to deliver this new value to its customers. If an organization doesn't or can't change, it will either go out of business or get swallowed by a more adaptable competitor.

In the early twentieth century, the city—which is really the business environment that the FDNY operates in—was changing. New technologies and trends led to all kinds of unprecedented emergencies that required the department's intervention. In 1915, for example, two hundred people were overcome by smoke in a subway fire, an event that was a real wake-up call for the department. Suddenly realizing that doing their job meant evolving to meet these new threats, the FDNY created the first rescue company. Under Captain John J. McElligott, Rescue 1 would soon become a kind of firefighting Delta Force, a crew of very experienced and talented firefighters, trained in the latest tools and technology, who could handle the unique emergencies of the world's most modern and rapidly growing city. Since then the special operations aspect of the FDNY has continued to expand, with rescue companies in all five boroughs now, in addition to the squads and dedicated haz-mat company, all incorporated under the Special Operations Command. In addition to being consummate firefighters, rescue guys are experts in building and bridge rappelling, scuba diving, subway car derailments, and antiterrorism warfare.

HOW CAN I LEAD FOR CHANGE?

Recognizing the need for change, initiating the process, and successfully managing the execution demands extraordinary leadership. When Lou Gerstner took over IBM in 1993, the company was well on its way to posting an $8 billion loss for the year. In fact, most of the business community thought that IBM couldn't survive in its current form and should be broken up. Gerstner agreed, up to a point. IBM, which at the time was an organization obsessed with its internal reality and lost in its glorious past, couldn't go on in its current form, but being broken up wasn't the remedy. Change, however, was.

There's no question that Gerstner actually chose the tougher option. Breaking a company into smaller pieces is, at least, a tangible activity. But producing real change in an organization the size of IBM is like wrestling with smoke. "You can't simply give a couple of speeches or write a new credo for the company and declare that a new culture has taken hold," Gerstner said, describing his approach. "The levers you have to pull are cultural, not directional. It's how people think, what they value, what they do."

At IBM, Gerstner was able to lead the organization through a major change that required people to redefine themselves and their company. This is by far the most daunting type of change, a six-alarm, "Yeah, we'll be working late on this one" kind of change. But the funny thing is, people will resist you almost as much for the small changes as they will for the big ones.

For instance, the firefighters in every firehouse buy their own food, sundries, and pretty much anything else they need, including appliances such as TVs and microwaves. Much of this comes out of something called the house tax. When I was a lieutenant in 18 Truck, the house tax was collected weekly and managed by the senior firefighter, which suited me just fine. Then when I became a captain, and moved to 48 Engine in the Bronx, I found that the custom there was for the company commander to handle the tax. That meant me. I wasn't crazy about this situation, basically because I felt it was a waste of my time. But I soon figured out that pushing this particular change was going to be an even bigger time suck. This is a perfect example of how fiercely people will sometimes resist even the smallest, most inconsequential changes.

And it's not just the people. For the most part, an organization's structure and processes are there to add stability and predictability; this means that the organization itself is constructed in such a way as to resist change. In addition to the forms, protocols, and all that stuff in the employee handbook, there's a ton of intangible qualities—such as an organization's values—that have to be accounted for if you're trying to spark a transformation.

Anything that threatens the familiar routine or requires people to think or act in new ways provokes resistance. This is because most of us want stability. The uncertainty caused by change leaves people feeling disoriented and powerless. Because of this, the key to managing change is making it seem not like work they *have* to do, but like work they *need* to do.

HOW TO MANAGE YOUR PEOPLE IN THE FACE OF CHANGE

So if people and organizations just naturally resist change, what can you possibly do to lead them through the process? Quite a lot, actually. The main reason that leaders have trouble pulling off change isn't that people are resistant—people are resistant to lots of things, but they'll still do them if you provide the right guidance—but that leaders mismanage the process.

Usually, by the time a manager gets around to talking to his people about the need for a change, the change itself has already been decided upon. To that manager's people, this makes change seem like something imposed on them, a punishment. Compounding the problem, this style of communication—informing or telling, rather than discussing—makes people feel helpless. They sense, rightfully so, that they have no control over their own destiny. So it's not surprising that they would perceive any change as a threat and react accordingly. We leaders sense their hostile vibe, and then consciously or unconsciously we begin to think of our own people as adversaries in the change process.

James MacGregor Burns said that leaders need to make people feel that they are the origins of a movement, not its pawns. Now before you think I've gone off the deep end and am telling you to let your people run the show, read that sentence carefully. It doesn't say that all decisions should come from your people, but that your people should *feel* as though they are a meaningful part of the decisions that affect them. And you already know from the chapters on trust and decision making several ways to make your people feel involved and significant.

Decision making and managing change have a great deal in common. Since change, when you think about it, is just a particular type of decision, this shouldn't come as a huge shock. Change is usually more difficult to execute, that's true, but deep down, change and decisions have the same DNA. And just as ownership and accountability lead to more effective decision making, they can also help you implement and manage change.

Once you decide that a change is necessary, the next thing you need to do is align your people with the need for that change and get them to take ownership for its execution. However, unlike the standard decision-making cycle, where your people really do have some voice in the process, when it comes time to implement the large, transforming types of changes, the decision to actually go ahead with a particular change has already been made. So what happens then?

HERE'S WHAT TO DO IF YOU WANT YOUR PEOPLE TO EMBRACE CHANGE

Don't think I'm being cynical when I tell you that you still need to make people feel like they're a part of the change process. Approach is everything here. I remember when I was a firefighter in Rescue 3. One of our company officers, Lieutenant Marty McTigue, walked in for his tour with what looked like a little duffel bag. Inside the bag was a new tool he'd discovered, an oddball little thing that was basically a hydraulic pump with a hose, and at the end of the hose, two tapered and shaped metal arms, hinged at one end, looking something like the ears of a rabbit. Turns out it was a hydraulic forcible-entry tool, in other words, a hydraulic device you could use to pop doors at a fire or other emergency. Now, this new tool the lieutenant had discovered—it was called a rabbit tool (I have no idea why)—presented the men of Rescue 3 with a problem.

You see, it's not like we'd been having any difficulty forcing doors up until that point. In fact, for about a hundred years we'd been applying axes or Halligan tools to just about anything with hinges and a knob, and been getting very satisfactory results. So our initial reaction was, "What do we need this for? We already know how to force doors." And Lieutenant McTigue, in his very low-key, soft-spoken way, said, "Gee, let's just put it on the rig. If we see a use for it, maybe we can pull it off and try and use the tool. You know, see how it works."

So Lieutenant McTigue asked me to put the tool on the rig, and I did. And the first run we had, we're heading out the door, and the tool somehow fell off the rig onto the apparatus floor. At least, that's how it seemed at the time. All I know for sure is, it wasn't there when we got to the job. Every time we came back to quarters, or every time Lieutenant McTigue worked, he would put it back on the rig again. And every time, it wouldn't be there when we'd show up at a fire. Strange, huh?

This went on for several weeks, until one time it actually made it to a fire, and it happened to be a job where we had a lot of doors to force. And someone grabbed it and brought it up and used it. And the thing worked incredibly well—very quickly, and with little chance of injury to the firefighters forcing the door. For you see, there *was* a problem with the way we'd been forcing doors. We were always smashing our fingers and hands with the tools due to the smoke, heat, and low visibility. Word spread quickly about our new toy, and to our surprise, within just a few months, companies that normally wouldn't even want to see us on the fire floor, because they wanted to handle things themselves, were calling us up. "Bring that rabbit tool up here, we've got a bunch of doors to force." So this thing grew in popularity very quickly. And now, every truck in the New York City Fire Department carries a hydraulic forcible-entry tool. It's an industry standard.

If you lead with the change, then that's what people will focus on. They'll drive themselves crazy thinking about what this particular change might mean for them, and then you'll spend all your time dealing with those fears instead of aligning your people with the need for change.

So try it a different way. Treat your people like adults and give them the information they need to evaluate the change on their own. Or as in the case of Lieutenant McTigue and his innovation, allow your people to uncover that information on their own. By doing so, you're implicitly including them in the process. A king never justifies his decisions to the peasants; by letting your people know that they're important enough to be included in the reasoning behind the decision, you assure them of their place inside the circle.

This should all seem kind of familiar, since it's really just transparency. Keeping that in mind, start talking to your people about events that are making the current change necessary. Use questions and teaching approaches to help your people see how these events are connected to your organization's health and longevity. Re-create the disorientation and uncertainty that inspired you or your bosses to decide to resolve the issue through change. Let your people experience the same sense of urgency and need that you felt when faced with these factors. Let them feel a little of the heat.

A fascinating case study featured in the *Harvard Business Review* looked at how change was managed at an elevator manufacturer the study's authors call Elco (not the company's real name). In the late 1980s, facing a diminishing market for their products along with other changes in their operating environment, Elco decided that if they wanted to stay competitive they needed to transform their manufacturing process. The company's leaders decided to roll out the new process at one of their premier plants, and to avoid upsetting or distracting the plant employees, didn't explain what would be happening or why. When they finally announced the change to the plant's employees, not only did they not explain the reason for the change, but the weeks of wild rumor concerning the mysterious business-suited strangers (the consultants that management hadn't wanted the employees to worry about) had taken their toll. The employees, suspicious of management's motives, rejected the initiative.

Meanwhile, at a plant whose history of management-labor friction led the company leaders to expect resistance, the plant manager introduced the consultants to the employees and went on to hold a series of meetings where he explained the company's motivation behind the change and made it relevant to the employees. These meetings were also opportunities for open discussion, where people could ask questions, raise issues, and offer ideas. In fact, the employees were encouraged to partner with the consultants—to become, in other words, part of the process. The fact that as a result of these measures, the plant's employees embraced the change and made it work validates the transparent, collaborative approach used by this manager.

As a leader, you not only have the power to control how your people perceive issues and to manage the pace at which they're forced to come to terms with them; you also have the ability to absorb and manage your followers' stress. (Remember in chapter 5, where I described how leaders can act as a holding environment for their people, helping them manage their stress until they can deal with a situation on their own?) Your ability to do this is rooted in the quality of the connections you've created with your people. The stronger those relationships and the more your people trust you, the more stress you'll be able to absorb.

A few years ago I would have talked mainly about how a fire officer acts as a holding environment when he and his company are actually attacking a fire. In that situation, when burning pieces of drywall and liquefied paint are drizzling down around you and the fire is pushing back hard, it's your officer's defiant stance and steady, reassuring words that allow you to move past your panic and stand firm.

But recently I learned that a leader can also serve as a holding environment in other ways. Working at Ground Zero, and also, during that same period, at the scene of the crash of flight 587 in Queens, we all saw things that we never thought we'd have to see. Certainly, firefighters are no strangers to violent death. I think all of us have witnessed what fire or collapse or high-speed impact can do to flesh and bone. But in both these instances the destruction was simply unthinkable. And it affected everyone. Consequently, I realized that more than ever, our men and women were looking to us, their leaders, for strength. And not just the strength to stay and keep working, but at times the strength to be able to leave the scene, to go off somewhere and collect themselves.

How does this work? We've already discussed how followers look to their leaders to define reality. And this is never more apparent than during times of turmoil and change. If the leader remains calm during these times, she's basically signaling to her followers that there's no reason to get excited, which helps them get their own feelings of anxiety under control. By using this phenomenon during times of change to manage your people's stress and keep them focused and engaged, you buy yourself the time you need to teach them about why the change is necessary and to align them with the initiative.

While your ability to serve as a holding environment helps you absorb and contain stress, it also allows you to give that stress back to your people. This lets you regulate the rate at which information reaches your people so they can process it without being overwhelmed by it and panicking. I know this all sounds a little strange, but think about it: because people look to you for meaning, the signals you send out are very potent. For example, this is why projecting an air of calm during stressful events neutralizes others' anxiety. In the same way, by showing just a little concern you can create useful stress that gets your followers' attention and focuses their energies while still keeping their anxiety within tolerable levels.

This is what allows you to align your people with the need for change. By framing information and parceling it out at a pace that your people can deal with, you can bring them to an understanding of why a change is necessary. Returning for a moment to the example I cited earlier involving the elevator company, it was because the second manager explained to his people the reasons for the change that he was able to get them to go along with it. Essentially, by giving them a chance to understand the *why* of a change—usually, that the change is necessary if the organization is to survive—you're also answering the question that must be addressed if you want to get people on board with something: "What's in it for me?"

EXECUTING CHANGE OVER THE LONG TERM

Getting your people on board with the change you have in mind is a tough challenge, but it's not the only one. Once you've gotten everyone aligned and committed, you still need to make sure the change happens. While for the most part you'll draw on the same methods and techniques that you use to support execution—such as setting milestones and giving people the freedom to achieve objectives in their own way—executing for change does present some unique challenges.

Your biggest obstacle when executing for change is time. The longer it takes for you to implement a change, the less the change will matter. According to Noel Tichy, if a change takes longer to implement than six months, it becomes absorbed into the normal routine of the organization. Somewhat ironically, this means that the change itself, and all the processes you've introduced to support that change (milestones and the like), become just another part of the company's bureaucracy. The initiative emerges as "just another thing to do, rather than a new way of doing things." A sense of urgency and the strong support of leaders and influencers at all levels of the organization are the things you'll need in order to overcome this subtle organizational assimilation.

The question is, how do you sustain the levels of engagement and enthusiasm your people will need in order to complete the initiative? Here are a few things you yourself can do to boost people's intensity and tempo:

- Set up a routine that forces you to circulate among your people.
- Be alert to opportunities to teach them about why the change is important.

- Devise a few stories that illustrate not only the need for change, but what the organization will look like once change has been accomplished, and tell these stories every chance you get.
- Project an optimistic and upbeat attitude.

In short, you need to be a cheerleader, a teacher, a true believer, and a bit of a bully.

The ability to manage change successfully has become something of a Holy Grail for all sorts of organizations over the past few years, and with good reason. That ability is one of the two competencies essential to leaders' ability to bring their companies through the uncertain times ahead. (Innovation is the other.) But the real edge these days is still leadership itself—not just the quality of leadership, but the quantity. By developing leaders throughout your organization you can execute a change initiative more effectively. But where do these leaders come from? And how can you get more of them?

Straight from the Chief

Leadership has always had an entrepreneurial aspect to it. Often, accomplishing your organization's objectives will require you to innovate some new way of providing value to your customers; or some change in your industry will mean that your organization needs to change as well. Since change is really just another type of decision that needs to be executed, many of the same methods you can use to help build accountability during the decision-making process will help you get people on board for your change initiative as well.

- Both innovation and change begin with following the smoke. And while innovation comes from insights into how to improve on something and provide better value, change demands that you have a clear-eyed appreciation for what's going on in your organization's environment and how it could impact your company.

- Innovation is not invention. Instead, it's the creation of a new kind of value, or a new way to deliver existing value. You can jump-start innovation by opening yourself up to new ideas and influences, and also by focusing on your customers and uncovering new ways to satisfy their needs.

- In order to get your people behind a change initiative, you'll need to somehow include them in the process. People resist change when it feels imposed on them, so you need to make them feel as if they have some control over what's happening to them.

CHAPTER II

Finding Your Top Whip

How can you develop leaders throughout
your organization? And how will this help you
be a more effective leader?

Every successful organization is built on layers of leaders, rather than held together by an all-powerful CEO, president, or chief of department. And while I've got a trove of gripping anecdotes that would show you how this network of leaders has saved the day during various emergencies, I'm not going to share them with you. Not because they're inaccurate or misleading—there's no question that these official and unofficial leaders are in large part responsible for our operational success—but because our leaders actually do their best and most important work during the quiet moments: meeting one-on-one with firefighters, teaching and mentoring probies, supporting a new officer in his first command, and upholding the traditions and values of the FDNY.

Throughout this book I've tried to show you examples that are dramatic as well as instructive. I've tried to show you how the same approaches we use to lead our people into a burning building or execute rescue operations in extreme circumstances will get results in any organization. But the truth is, most leadership—and this is as applicable in the FDNY as it is in GE, IBM, or Southwest Airlines—happens very quietly. Leadership is the result of thousands of little interactions, innovations, and decisions, all undertaken with a focus on the organization's mission.

Without the department's emphasis on developing leadership through the ranks, I probably wouldn't be commanding a battalion right now. When I first made lieutenant and was transferred out of Rescue 3 and eventually into 18 Truck, I had only seven and a half years of experience as a firefighter. Granted, I'd worked in some busy houses, and rescue experience counts for a lot, but nonetheless—had I experienced every kind of fire? did I know every possible way things could go wrong, or how to respond to every emergency? Well, no. And what's more, I was far less experienced than the men I was commanding. The truck chauffeur, for instance, had thirty-five years. At any given fire, nearly a hundred years of experience would jump off the rig. Guys with twenty years, twenty-three years, twenty-five years, eighteen years. My seven and a half were looking pretty meager.

But did these firefighters see me as inferior to them? Did they feel I'd usurped their position, or stolen a job that was rightfully theirs? Were they threatened by me? No. To some degree, this was because of the Test. They knew what I'd gone though to get to lieutenant, and this afforded me some credibility and respect. But mostly it was because the men of 18 Truck—particularly the senior men, or top whips—were already leaders in their own right, and they supported me.

The term *top whip* (or *whip*) is a throwback to the days when the apparatus would career through the city streets behind a team of horses, usually driven by the most senior and experienced firefighter. That firefighter was the top whip. This is not an official leadership position; you can't get promoted to top whip or put it on your résumé. But in terms of real authority and significance, the top whip is the equivalent of a master sergeant or master chief, depending on whether you root for the army or the navy; regardless of which branch of the service you side with, he's basically the guy who keeps the machinery humming.

These unofficial leaders are the backbone of the FDNY. There's even a saying that the senior men run the firehouse but are kind enough to let the officers work there. And to a large degree, this is true. The senior men uphold the traditions and codes, not just of their own house but of the entire department. They make the firehouses work. They ensure that maintenance gets done, and that everyone pulls his weight. It's the rare personnel problem that actually makes its way to my office, the whips are so effective at managing our people and resolving problems before they can become *my* problems.

But they don't accomplish this through fear or intimidation. And they don't do it because they have to—instead, they do it because they feel responsible for the success of the organization. Ray Pfeifer, a firefighter in 40 Engine, still remembers one of his first fires, and how the company's senior man looked out for him. Pfeifer was on the nozzle, which is a pretty demanding job even for experienced firefighters. As he remembers it, a wall of flame seemed to be coming right for him. He was very nervous, uncertain about what to do. But then an incredibly strong arm came around him from behind as the senior man, Bruce Gary, lifted him into position and began to carry him forward. Gary steadily propelled the younger man into the fire, shaking the long stream of water out before them. Pfeifer still recalls how Gary's calm, confident air settled over him, sweeping away his doubt and panic and reminding him that he knew what to do. After they'd knocked down the fire and Pfeifer turned to thank the man, Gary just smiled and told him, "You did okay, kid. Welcome to the New York City Fire Department."

Every firefighter could probably tell you a similar story. When I first started in 11 Truck, the top whip there, Richie Barto, had a tremendous impact on me, a very positive impact. He was constantly testing me, probing for my strengths and weaknesses, not to harass me but to figure out how he could help me improve. He made sure I was doing things right, whether it was remembering to gas up the saw before a tour or being careful not to lose my way in a smoke-drenched apartment. I always felt better if I knew I'd be working with Richie on an upcoming tour. I trusted him because I knew, even if it sometimes felt like he was riding me, that he was doing it because he sincerely wanted me to be the best firefighter possible.

Seven and a half years later, as a new lieutenant a few blocks away in 18 Truck, I found myself still relying on the whips for help and guidance. Yes, I was their lieutenant—they followed my orders and called me "Lou" for short—but they were the ones who supported me and helped me succeed as a young officer.

How did they do this? By helping me understand the particular culture of 18 Truck. By letting me know when a personnel matter needed my attention, and when the firefighters would work it out on their own. By giving me the benefit of their years of experience, both in the firehouse and on the fire ground, and helping me navigate the department's bureaucracy. Essentially, they saw it as their job to help me succeed. No one told them to do this. But the FDNY's culture of leadership had instilled in them these behaviors and values, and over time they became part of these firefighters' professional character. In fact, they had absorbed these standards from the top whips who'd tutored them in the ways of the department, and now they were handing them down to the probies and new leaders like myself.

Can you imagine this happening in your organization? A new leader comes in knowing that there's already a leadership network in place to support and help her succeed? Wouldn't that be great? Wouldn't that help her become a more effective leader?

This is why the third commitment focuses on the need to develop this system of leaders. These are the people who support all of an organization's key endeavors. They circulate new initiatives throughout the company, drive execution, alert others to opportunities for innovation, uncover reality, and funnel information to those whose lofty positions limit their frontline perspective. But helping others unlock their leadership potential is not easy.

So how is it done? Should you go out and encourage your people to boss one another around? No, of course not, because—remember—leadership has nothing to do with things like title, office, or executive perks. According to our definition, anyone who works through others to achieve the organization's objectives is, technically, a leader. Which means that the customer service rep who takes new hires under her wing to teach them how to serve their customers is a leader. And so is the shipping clerk who organizes his colleagues to help streamline the fulfillment process, and the senior firefighter who brings everyone together to build a new training area in the firehouse basement. These people, and thousands of other modest, unofficial leaders in organizations across the country, are getting things done without the benefit of a C-level title.

Ironically, these unofficial leaders are often marginalized and branded as troublemakers by their organizations. Though this happens most frequently in places that confuse leadership with rank, it can occur anywhere. Why? Because even though these under-the-radar leaders are acting in the best interests of their organizations, their ideas and innovations are seen as provocations, attempts to upset the status quo and make life a hassle for everyone. This is why part of developing leaders throughout your organization means protecting these unsung leaders from harm. You need to provide cover for their ideas and support them if you see them clashing with the entrenched self-interest of others in the company.

RECOGNIZING THE
LEADERSHIP POTENTIAL AROUND YOU

But developing leaders doesn't mean prepping them for promotion; instead, it's about encouraging a particular set of qualities and attitudes.

Before you start trying to develop leaders, you first need to identify the qualities you feel are necessary for leadership. Leadership isn't something that anyone, regardless of his or her strengths and weaknesses, can learn. Unless you don't mind wasting your time on people with little or no aptitude for it, you've got to figure out how to select only the most likely leadership candidates.

Start by zeroing in on the strengths that seem to you to support effective leadership. How do you find these? By studying other successful leaders, both the ones you work with and those you encounter in books and through seminars. For me, the ideal leader is someone who's

- deeply committed to the organization's mission
- truly enthusiastic about leading
- driven by more than ego gratification
- eager and able to tackle hard, challenging work
- capable of learning new things

I've found that as long as someone has these strengths as a foundation, I'm usually able to help the person develop any missing skills or neutralize any self-sabotaging blind spots. I'm not really so arrogant, though, as to think that my humble list of leadership qualities is the last word. It's possible that your own list will be completely different, and yet just as meaningful. The only hard and fast rule, I think, is that you should select for strengths ("good-at's") rather than for skills or experience.

Sometimes potential leaders won't even seem like worthwhile employees. Their strengths will appear to be weaknesses or, frankly, irritations. Not long ago, a young officer called me to ask my advice about one of the firefighters in his company. Apparently this firefighter was always questioning the way this officer was going about things, or trying to get involved in areas that weren't really part of his official job description. This is always a tough situation, and there's no standard fix for it. On the one hand, you can certainly lower the boom on this guy, and explain to him who the boss is and what exactly the boss expects. You're the chief. This is without question a legitimate and effective way to handle someone who doesn't recognize your authority. And while sometimes this is the only way—believe me—the problem I have with this approach is, it doesn't really resolve the issue. There's something more going on with these characters, either a bad job fit or a bad career fit, and by constantly hammering this person down you're neglecting the more important part of leadership, that is, building your other people up.

So the other possible approach is to look at his behavior and ask yourself: Are there strengths here that I'm overlooking? Can I somehow channel this person's obvious enthusiasm, ideas, and energy into productive work? If a guy really thinks he's got something to contribute to your organization, you might be better off giving him a chance to make that contribution. You could call him and say, "You know what? You seem like you're really involved and have a lot of energy and a lot of ideas. I have a couple of things I need some help with. Can you help me?" When you're the chief, nobody ever says no to "Can you help me?" And once you accepts your offer, he's yours. He's working for you again.

HELP YOUR NEW LEADERS GROW

As you start assessing your people's leadership potential, you'll discover that some of them have what it takes to lead but aren't in a position to actually do anything about it. For example, an employee who doesn't need to rely very much on others to do his job hasn't had a lot of opportunities to exercise leadership, though he may have all the qualities you're looking for. So how can you see if this person has the ability to translate that potential into actual leadership?

In many organizations, people who are successful in one role and show some leadership potential are often "developed" by being promoted to a management position. This isn't so much development as it is gambling, or maybe wishful thinking. All you've done is put a person in a totally new and very demanding position, and then asked him to learn this unforgiving role as he performs it (not that that's even possible). You've also put yourself in a difficult position. What's likely to happen is that he will be unprepared for the nature and demands of his new job. He'll falter, develop bad habits, and alienate his people, and then where are you? You don't want to get rid of a good person, but you can't demote him back to the role he excelled at. You and the organization are now stuck with a bad manager.

Fortunately, you can develop your people without promoting them outright. For instance, you can provide someone with a temporary leadership experience by placing her in charge of executing a special initiative or leading a new project or guiding a group in carrying out some special assignment (like my assignment to create a training curriculum for the academy). Make her accountable for the results, but stay engaged and meet with her regularly to discuss her progress. Don't come down on her for her inevitable mistakes, but use those mistakes as opportunities for teaching. At the same time, you can assess her leadership aptitude without being forced into a make-or-break decision; when the project is over, the person will return to her full-time position.

While I believe that this is a great way to develop your people and expose them to new challenges, there are a few things you need to watch out for. First, when establishing the project, make it clear to the group that your leadership candidate is authorized to lead. What she accomplishes with that authority is up to her, but if you don't at least make it clear to the group who's in charge, you're setting your person up for failure, big-time. Second, make sure your person is equal to the opportunity. Translation? Don't throw her into the deep end unless you know she can swim. A project or initiative that's too demanding for a person's particular experience or skill level will crush her confidence and set her development back years. At least initially, select projects that are within your person's range of experience and that don't have a lot riding on her success or failure.

DON'T MOLD PEOPLE, MENTOR THEM

Another means of developing leaders is mentoring. My sense is that mentoring has already passed in and out of favor in management circles, and I've even read some books that dismiss it entirely. And yet, mentoring has proven to be very effective in the fire department in terms of preparing up-and-coming leaders for the demands of a position. While we have formal and informal mentoring, they're both so thoroughly supported by our culture and professional traditions that there's really no difference between the two. In fact, I believe that our embrace of mentoring contributes significantly to the high quality of the FDNY's leadership corps.

But what is mentoring anyway? It's one of those terms that gets thrown around a lot, and I think everyone has an idea of what it means, but I've encountered few people who could confidently define it. Mentoring, as we refer to it in the department, is simply teaching and transparency. It means allowing someone to assume the role of student, and then answering his questions and letting him observe how you do your job. It means explaining things using a context he's familiar with. For instance, when I'm mentoring a captain who aspires to be a battalion chief, I'll couch things in terms of situations I know a captain would recognize. *Mentoring* is really a fancy word for *teaching*. It's more focused perhaps, but that's really about it.

As I mentioned earlier, in the FDNY we have formal and informal mentoring. The formal mentoring kicks in at the captain's level during the process of testing and evaluating them for the chief officer level. The transition from company officer to chief officer is much different from, say, the transition from lieutenant to captain or even from firefighter to lieutenant. You're no less of a leader at the company level, of course—you certainly need to be aware of your environment, plan for the future, and develop your people—but you're focused primarily on your company or firehouse. At the chief officer level, you're responsible for much more. You need to be aware of the big picture and how it affects what you're doing at any given moment. Your decisions carry greater weight. There are far more resources at your disposal, and you must to learn to wield these effectively. Overall, your job is more complex and requires a different leadership approach, which is why we have an official program that rotates captains among a series of battalion chiefs, thus giving them the chance to learn from people who probably have a variety of leadership styles.

While there's no official program for mentoring lieutenants as they make the jump to captain, or firefighters as they move up to the company officer level, because our values promote teaching and mentoring you won't find a company officer who doesn't also serve as a mentor to his people. This is so deeply ingrained in us—drilled into us, in fact, by those who mentored us when we came on the job—that I'm not even sure we're always aware of what's going on. We rely so heavily on teaching to pass on valuable skills and knowledge, induct probies into the FDNY's unique culture, improve our abilities, and form strong relationships, that mentoring is just naturally adopted as a complementary behavior.

FITTING YOUR ORGANIZATION
FOR A LEADERSHIP PIPELINE

Part of the rationale behind developing leaders at all levels is that it creates the foundation for what's referred to as a "leadership pipeline." This is one of those rare management terms that actually means what it sounds like: a leadership pipeline describes any kind of process within your organization that is geared toward the selection and development of leaders. One of the biggest problems faced by organizations today is their lack of homegrown talent. On the other hand, one of the great strengths of the FDNY is our leadership pipeline. All of our leaders have come up through the ranks. This ensures a rare continuity in terms of familiarity with the organizational culture. And this is really the point of developing an in-house leadership pipeline; it ensures that your organization will have access to leaders who really understand its character and mission, and who are therefore in the best position to come into a top management role and be effective.

A leadership pipeline, however, doesn't come about through good intentions. Instead, it's the result of a disciplined approach that includes processes for evaluating your people and identifying potential leaders; developing those leaders; and assessing their eligibility for higher positions in the organization. To that end, I want to just share with you some guidelines I use in my own leadership prospecting.

First, the info you gather as you interact with and observe your people will help you evaluate their leadership potential. When you think you've identified a possible candidate, create a file for him where you'll keep your notes. These should be a record of each person's key successes and failures, as well as examples of his strengths and weaknesses so you can refer to them during reviews. These notes will also help you devise a leadership development plan for each person that's tailored to his specific needs. This is not as big a deal as it may sound: my "leadership development plans" tend to be a few lines scribbled on notepaper, usually about how a certain person needs to develop his communication skills or his coaching abilities. Using my notes to guide me, I will try to create between two and four leadership opportunities for the person each year, opportunities that somehow relate to the skills, techniques, or strengths he needs to develop.

Now, I don't want you to go out there and try to put these methods to work only to get discouraged by the inherent messiness of the whole process. As I've outlined it here it seems pretty easy, requiring nothing more of you than that you wait for your high-potential people to volunteer themselves, and then point out their key strengths and leadership qualities. In the real world, however, it could take years for you to discover a person's leadership potential. At the same time, other employees will seem like natural leaders right off the bat, except that months or years down the road, the development process will expose some critical weaknesses. One way to improve your batting average is to discuss your candidates with other leaders—both official and unofficial—who might have worked with them. Get their perspectives on your prospect's capabilities. Compare notes and listen to what they have to say. As in any situation, you need other points of view in order to compensate for your own blind spots.

In fact, the most important person you should consult is your top whip. One of the first things I did when I became captain of 48 Engine—and I suggest it to friends and students of mine who make captain or lieutenant—was to seek out the whips. I sat down and talked with them. The whips represent a tremendous source of knowledge and insight. They know where the company's been. They know who all the people are. They know who was there last, when they left, and what's going on. They know what's been tried before, what worked and didn't work, and why.

On the other hand, I know that not every organization has committed itself to cultivating the leadership spirit among its rank and file. There are all kinds of reasons why this might be—and few (if any) of them have anything to do with malice or ignorance. Instead, I think it's because during the frenzy of day-to-day operations, leadership development seems like the last thing you have time to focus on. Nevertheless, if your organization has let leadership development slide, it's up to you to pick up the slack. If your organization doesn't already have a network of whips, then you'll have to create one.

Start by actually designating someone to be your strong right hand.

The ideal top whip is someone who's experienced, respected, loyal (to you and the organization), and whose leadership style and perspective complement your own. A sycophant or yes-man is not a top whip. While it's tempting to choose a right hand who shares your own views on things, you'll find that he'll be most valuable if his strengths complement your weaknesses and if his point of view is different from your own.

Given all that, the most important thing you should look for in a top whip is honesty. You want a whip who gives you the straight story, all the time, no matter how much it may contradict your own take on things. If the person you've chosen as your right hand isn't used to a manager who really wants to hear what he thinks, you may have to prove to him that you're for real. But by now, you know how this works: encourage the straight talk you want by, first, asking for it, and then—so he knows that you value his candor—listening carefully and accounting for his perspective in your final decision.

Developing leaders throughout your organization is hardly something that can be accomplished overnight. While it's possible on your own to develop a network of unofficial leaders—a corps of whips in your corner of the organizational universe—since it requires you to develop a value system and culture that supports these leaders, it's more likely to happen if you can get the backing of the company's top executives. Once they're on board, you can begin to cultivate the type of environment that promotes leadership at all levels.

Straight from the Chief

Until you develop a network of leaders who can mobilize their fellow employees in support of your decisions, your leadership will always fall short of its potential. Whether these leaders hold an official rank or title, or simply work through others to get things done, these people are the key to an agile, thriving organization.

- You can help develop leaders throughout your organization by determining what you feel are the essential leadership qualities, figuring out who among your people exhibit these qualities, and then guiding them into temporary leadership positions.

- Unofficial leaders are the ones who make life difficult for all those who settle for "good enough." They raise difficult questions and challenge outdated assumptions. Protect these people and help them grow, or they'll get squashed by the guardians of the status quo.

- Find an influential person you can trust and recruit him to be your top whip. A top whip, or strong right hand, will give you honest feedback, serve as a reliable source of information, and rally support for your initiatives.

Conclusion

I live in a small town north of the city. The town's name is Blooming Grove. A fair number of firefighters live there, and consequently, that community was one of those for whom the shock and pain of September 11 ran particularly deep.

The town resolved that a monument should be built to honor the firefighters who lost their lives in the attacks, and I served on the committee that oversaw its planning and implementation. The memorial was finished in the summer of 2002, and soon after its dedication, a friend and I arranged to meet there before going on to do whatever it was we had planned for that day. It was bright, and mild for August, and seemed to be one of the few times that summer when it wasn't raining. We were sitting in a small alcove that was part of the monument, and my friend, who wasn't a firefighter, asked me why so many of the firefighters whose names were carved into the memorial tablets were officers, and not just lieutenants and captains, but battalion chiefs and deputy chiefs.

First in, last out. As I sat there looking at the names, trying to think of how best to answer my friend's question, I realized how completely that phrase sums up the leadership philosophy of the FDNY. It's the guiding principle behind everything we do. It speaks to our love for our men and our commitment to give them the best leadership possible. It speaks to how highly we value the job we do and the people we serve. We don't stand behind our people, or put ourselves above them. We lead out front, where everyone can see us.

My friend was waiting for an answer, so I explained to him that in the FDNY, officers lead their men into battle and then stand and fight alongside them. And we all leave together—or we don't leave at all. And even in death our names are etched side-by-side with theirs, eternally honoring that commitment to stand by our men no matter what.

Notes

Chapter 1. You're the Chief

The Fiorella La Guardia quote comes from Terry Golway's welcome history of the FDNY, *So Others Might Live*. For essential insight into the nature of organizations, you still can't beat Peter Drucker. For this section I turned to his *The Essential Drucker*. I also benefited from the elegant, concise analysis of organizations provided by Joan Magretta and Nan Stone in their book *What Management Is*. The New York City and FDNY statistics came from the FDNY's own annual report. James MacGregor Burns's book *Leadership*, as well as Warren Bennis's *On Becoming a Leader* and Ronald A. Heifetz's *Leadership Without Easy Answers*, offers rigorous and inspired definitions of what it means to be a leader.

Chapter 2. The Leadership Triangle

Vincent Dunn's *Command and Control of Fires and Emergencies* contains helpful passages on the aggressive nature of fire, as well as examples of the importance of gathering information. In their book *Execution*, Larry Bossidy and Ram Charan highlight the need for leaders to ferret out the underlying reality in order to make effective business decisions. Drucker describes the different kinds of information available to managers in *The Essential Drucker*. In their book *Shackleton's Way*, Margot Morrell and Stephanie Capparell use the leadership style of Sir Ernest Shackleton to illustrate the usefulness of one's followers in uncovering information. Many of these authors emphasize the need to be a teacher as well as a manager, particularly Noel Tichy in *The Cycle of Leadership*. The Jack Welch quote on developing people also comes from Tichy's book. Golway scrupulously reconstructs early New York City firefighting in *So Others Might Live*. In *First, Break All the Rules*, Marcus Buckingham and Curt Coffman discuss the importance of putting the right person to the right job. Check out James MacGregor Burns's *Leadership* for some particularly interesting insights into how leaders can lead only through the support of those below them.

Chapter 3. Fueling the Leadership Fire

Golway again delivers the great stories of New York City's early firefighters. Turn to Warren Bennis for a clear-eyed discussion of the social aspects of leadership. Bossidy and Charan helped me understand how my own leadership practices—particularly the techniques I use to track and improve my leadership—could be useful to a broader audience. *Primal Leadership*, by Daniel Goleman, Richard Boyatzis, and Annie McKee, offers an invaluable perspective on the role of self-awareness and self-management in leadership. The quote on how the Marine Corps can learn from the FDNY's leadership approach is from Capt. Lawrence A. Colby's article, "New York's Bravest: Real World, Real Pressure."

Chapter 4. Don't Waste Your Water on Smoke

Many books discuss the importance of clarifying your organization's mission and values, but you can't go wrong with Peter Drucker's treatment of the subject, or Joan Magretta and Nan Stone's in their *What Management Is*. The quote from Battalion Chief Ed Schoales can be found in Dennis Smith's invaluable chronicle, *Report from Ground Zero*.

Chapter 5. Every Chief Needs a Radio, a White Helmet, and His People's Trust

Golway offers a gripping recounting of the 1993 bombing of the World Trade Center. Heifetz, though his book is not exactly easy reading, offers some incisive observations of how leaders create a safe environment within which their people can work. Goleman, Boyatzis, and McKee discuss the importance of transparency in their book *Primal Leadership*. The film shot by Jules and Gedeon Naudet at the Trade Center on 9/11 contains some vivid and moving examples of FDNY leadership. Peter Drucker has talked about how stories can be used to bolster one's leadership.

Chapter 6. Know Their Names Before You Send Them into the Flames

The Richard Picciotto quote is from his account of the World Trade Center attack, *Last Man Down*. The quote about leaders needing to make productive the strengths and knowledge of each individual is from Peter Drucker (the italics are mine), as are the stats about communication. Many people have spoken about using your people's goals as a basis for management, but no one's nailed it quite the way Drucker has; his insights helped me put a name to what we've been doing for years in the department. Goleman et al. confirmed with research what I'd always observed, which is that a positive attitude boosts people's ability to come up with creative solutions. I also use here his term, *dissonance,* to describe what happens when a leader is out of sync with his people. The Abraham Lincoln quote is from Donald T. Phillips's *Lincoln on Leadership*.

Chapter 7. Making the Right Call When the Heat Is On

Golway profiles several of the department's early, pivotal officers, and also offers excellent details on Bob Bohack's experience on 9/11. The Michael Dell quote comes from Tichy's *The Cycle of Leadership*. Donald Rumsfeld's leadership style is featured in a March 19, 2003, *New York Times* article by Thom Shanker and Eric Schmitt. The James Burke quote comes from Bennis's *On Becoming a Leader*. Some of you might recognize elements of Colonel John Boyd's decision-making process here (and for those of you who've never heard of Boyd, he was a fighter pilot who wrote the book on modern air combat tactics, among other things). I used to teach decision making in a slightly different way, but when I encountered Boyd's approach I realized it said what I was saying, only better, so I adopted it. (That's another leadership lesson: never be afraid to borrow a best practice, no matter where you find it!) Jason Santamaria and Vincent Martino's *The Marine Corps Way* offers an excellent overview of leadership strategies innovated by the marine corps and other military organizations.

Chapter 8. No One Goes Home Until the Fire's Out

Vincent Dunn's description of how he followed priorities on the fire ground comes from his book. The Larry Bossidy and Ram Charan quote on the importance of follow-through after a decision is taken is from their book. If you're interested in delving deeper into the subject of execution, I certainly recommend their book, as well as Peter Drucker, who has touched on many of the same points. The details on Welch's CEC process and the Special Forces' after-action review come from Tichy.

Chapter 9. Fire Up Your People's Performance

The quote about making your organization's goals tangible in order to manage for results is from Drucker. The reference to sociologists' discovery that people value similar qualities, regardless of culture, comes from Burns's *Leadership*. Once again, Golway provides vital historical background on the department.

Chapter 10. The Fire You Beat Today Is Not the One You'll Face Tomorrow

The Damon Knight quote is from his book *Creating Short Fiction*. The requirements for the successful implementation of an innovation come from Drucker, who has written a huge amount of fascinating material on the subject. The Warren Bennis quote is from his book. The story of Lou Gerstner's revival of IBM is from *Knowledge@ Wharton*'s article "Lou Gerstner's Turnaround Tales at IBM" and from "Gerstner Describes Bringing IBM Back to Health," by Joyce Routson, posted November 19, 2002, on the Stanford Graduate School of Business Web site. The Elco case study comes from the 1997 *Harvard Business Review* article "Fair Process: Managing in the Knowledge

Economy," by W. Chan Kim and Renée Mauborgne. I draw Tichy's ideas about the speed with which changes need to be implemented from his book.

Chapter 11. Finding Your Top Whip

The exchange between Bruce Gary and Ray Pfeifer comes from David Halberstam's touching, stoic book on the men of 40 Engine and 35 Ladder, *Firehouse*.

Bibliography

Abrashoff, D. Michael. *It's Your Ship*. New York: Warner Books, 2002.

Bennis, Warren. *On Becoming a Leader*. Cambridge: Perseus, 1989.

Bossidy, Larry, and Ram Charan. *Execution: The Discipline of Getting Things Done*. New York: Crown Business, 2002.

Buckingham, Marcus, and Curt Coffman. *First, Break All the Rules: What the World's Greatest Managers Do Differently*. New York: Simon & Schuster, 1999.

Burns, James MacGregor. *Leadership*. New York: Harper, 1978.

Colby, Lawrence A. "New Yorker's Bravest: Real World, Real Pressure," *Marine Corps Gazette*, December 2001.

Drucker, Peter F. *The Essential Drucker*. New York: HarperBusiness, 2001.

Dunn, Vincent. *Command and Control of Fires and Emergencies*. Saddle Brook, N.J.: Fire Engineering, 1999.

Goleman, Daniel, Richard Boyatzis, and Annie McKee. *Primal Leadership: Realizing the Power of Emotional Intelligence*. Boston: Harvard Business School Press, 2000.

Golway, Terry. *So Others Might Live: A History of New York's Bravest: The FDNY from 1700 to the Present*. New York: Basic Books, 2002.

Flynn, Sean. *3,000 Degrees: The True Story of a Deadly Fire and the Men Who Fought It*. New York: Warner Books, 2002.

Halberstam, David. *Firehouse*. New York: Hyperion, 2002.

Harari, Oren. *The Leadership Secrets of Colin Powell*. New York: McGraw-Hill, 2002.

Heifetz, Ronald A. *Leadership Without Easy Answers*. Cambridge: Harvard University Press, 1994.

Kim, W. Chan, and Renée Mauborgne. "Fair Process: Managing in the Knowledge Economy," *Harvard Business Review*, 1997; reprint, January 2003.

Knight, Damon. *Creating Short Fiction*. Cincinnati: Writer's Digest Books, 1981.

Magretta, Joan, with Nan Stone. *What Management Is: How It Works and Why It's Everyone's Business*. New York: Free Press, 2002.

Morrell, Margot, and Stephanie Capparell. *Shackleton's Way: Leadership Lessons from the Great Antarctic Explorer*. New York: Penguin, 2001.

Phillips, Donald T. *Lincoln on Leadership*. New York: Warner Books, 1992.

Picciotto, Richard, with Daniel Paisner. *Last Man Down*. New York: Berkley Books, 2002.

Santamaria, Jason, Vincent Martino, and Eric K. Clemons, Ph.D. *The Marine Corps Way: Using Manuever Warfare to Lead a Winning Organization*. New York: McGraw-Hill, 2003.

Shanker, Thom, and Eric Schmitt. "Rumsfeld Seeks Consensus Through Jousting," *New York Times,* March 19, 2003.

Smith, Dennis. *Report from Engine Co. 82*. New York: Warner Books, 1972.

————. *Report from Ground Zero*. New York: Viking, 2002.

Tichy, Noel M., with Nancy Cardwell. *The Cycle of Leadership: How Great Leaders Teach Their Companies to Win*. New York: HarperBusiness, 2002.

Useem, Michael. *The Leadership Moment: Nine True Stories of Triumph and Disaster and Their Lessons for Us All*. New York: Times Books, 1998.

Index